U.S. POSTAGE 3¢
SOUTH DAKOTA
U.S. POSTAGE
4¢
NEW MEXICO STATEHOOD
U.S. POSTAGE
OREGON TERRITORY CENTENNIAL
1912 ARIZONA 1962
U.S. POSTAGE 4¢
OHIO SESQUICENTENNIAL
1803 1953
UNITED STATES POSTAGE
U.S. POSTAGE
1636 1936
WASHINGTON
Stone Mountain Memorial
NEBRASKA STATEHOOD
1867-1967
U.S. POSTAGE 5¢
JULY 4, 1960
4¢
U.S. POSTAGE
SAN JUAN, PUERTO RICO
1521-1971
ILLINOIS 1818 1968
6¢ U.S. POSTAGE
INDIANA
1816 1966
5¢
U.S. POSTAGE
NEW HAMPSHIRE
LIVE FREE OR DIE
1876 COLORADO
WISCONSIN
CENTENNIAL
UNITED STATES
MINNESOTA TERRITORIAL CENTENNIAL
1849 1949
ALABAMA
1819 1969
UNITED STATES
1620 THE LANDING OF THE PILGRIMS
U.S.POSTAGE 6 CENTS
STEPHEN WATTS KEARNY EXPEDITION
1846 ENTRY INTO SANTA FE 1946
WEST VIRGINIA
5¢
6¢
WILDLIFE CONSERVATION
TEXAS CENTENNIAL
1836-1936
Missouri 1821-1971 United States 8¢
UNITED STATES POSTAGE 3¢
U.S. POSTAGE
1890 1940
THREE 3 CENTS
NEW JERSEY TERCENTENARY
1664 1964
6¢
ARKANSAS RIVER NAVIGATION
HAWAII STATEHOOD 1959
U.S. AIR MAIL 7¢
FORT TICONDEROGA
UNITED STATES POSTAGE
1812-1962
LOUISIANA
4¢
U.S. POSTAGE
UNITED STATES POSTAGE
3¢
THE MACKINAC BRIDGE
CHEROKEE STRIP
UNITED STATES POSTAGE 6¢
MAINE STATEHOOD
1820-1970
U.S.POSTAGE SIX CENTS
OREGON STATEHOOD
1859 1959
U.S. POSTAGE 4 CENTS
Carolina Charter
1663-1963
5 cents
U.S. postage
CALIFORNIA
1769 1969
United States 6 cents
TEXAS
KANSAS STATEHOOD 1861-1961
4¢
U.S. POSTAGE
CONNECTICUT
1635 1935
SOUTH CAROLINA
1670 1970
6¢
MISSISSIPPI
1817 1967
U.S. POSTAGE 5¢
1815
BATTLE OF NEW ORLEANS
GREAT NORTHWEST
1820 FORT SNELLING 1970
US 6¢
SEATTLE WORLD'S FAIR 1962
UNITED STATES POSTAGE
4¢
UNITED STATES POSTAGE
3¢
1792 1942
U.S. AIR MAIL
7¢
ALASKA STATEHOOD
NEVADA
1864 1964
STATEHOOD
U.S. POSTAGE
5¢

LINCOLN
Libby
FLATHEAD
Kalispell
GLACIER
Cut Bank
TOOLE
Shelby
LIBERTY
Chester
HILL
Havre
Chinook
BLAINE
Malta
PHILLIPS
VALLEY
Glasgow
Scobey
DANIELS
Plentywood
SHERIDAN
ROOSEVELT
Wolf Point
PONDERA
Conrad
SANDERS
Thompson Falls
LAKE
Polson
TETON
Choteau
CHOUTEAU
Fort Benton
RICHLAND
Sidney
MINERAL
Superior
MISSOULA
Missoula
POWELL
LEWIS AND CLARK
Great Falls
CASCADE
MC CONE
Circle
Jordan
GARFIELD
DAWSON
Glendive
Stanford
JUDITH BASIN
FERGUS
Lewistown
Winnett
PETROLEUM
WIBAUX
Wibaux
HELENA
PRAIRIE
Terry
Hamilton
RAVALLI
GRANITE
Philipsburg
Deer Lodge
MEAGHER
White Sulphur Springs
WHEATLAND
Harlowton
GOLDEN VALLEY
Ryegate
MUSSELSHELL
Roundup
ROSEBUD
Forsyth
Miles City
CUSTER
Baker
FALLON
Anaconda
Boulder
JEFFERSON
BROADWATER
Townsend
Butte
SILVER BOW
Hysham
TREASURE
YELLOWSTONE
Billings
Big Timber
SWEET GRASS
STILLWATER
Columbus
Hardin
BIG HORN
Ekalaka
CARTER
BEAVERHEAD
Dillon
MADISON
Virginia City
GALLATIN
Bozeman
Livingston
PARK
CARBON
Red Lodge
Broadus
POWDER RIVER
YELLOWSTONE NATIONAL PARK

The New

Enchantment of America

MONTANA

By Allan Carpenter

CHILDRENS PRESS, CHICAGO

ACKNOWLEDGMENTS

For assistance in the preparation of the revised edition, the author thanks:
The TRAVEL PROMOTION UNIT, MONTANA DEPARTMENT OF HIGHWAYS.

American Airlines—Anne Vitaliano, Director of Public Relations; *Capitol Historical Society*, Washington, D. C. ; *Newberry Library*, Chicago, Dr. Lawrence Towner, Director; *Northwestern University Library*, Evanston, Illinois; *United Airlines*—John P. Grember, Manager of Special Promotions; Joseph P. Hopkins, Manager, News Bureau; Carl Provorse, *Carpenter Publishing House*.

UNITED STATES GOVERNMENT AGENCIES: *Department of Agriculture*—Robert Hailstock, Jr., Photography Division, Office of Communication; Donald C. Schuhart, Information Division, Soil Conservation Service. *Army*—Doran Topolosky, Public Affairs Office, Chief of Engineers, Corps of Engineers. *Department of Interior*—Louis Churchville, Director of Communications; EROS Space Program—Phillis Wiepking, Community Affairs; Charles Withington, Geologist; Mrs. Ruth Herbert, Information Specialist; Bureau of Reclamation; National Park Service—Fred Bell and the individual sites; Fish and Wildlife Service—Bob Hines, Public Affairs Office. *Library of Congress*—Dr. Alan Fern, Director of the Department of Research; Sara Wallace, Director of Publications; Dr. Walter W. Ristow, Chief, Geography and Map Division; Herbert Sandborn, Exhibits Officer. *National Archives*—Dr. James B. Rhoads, Archivist of the United States; Albert Meisel, Assistant Archivist for Educational Programs; David Eggenberger, Publications Director; Bill Leary, Still Picture Reference; James Moore, Audio-Visual Archives. *United States Postal Service*—Herb Harris, Stamps Division.

For assistance in the preparation of the first edition, the author thanks:
Dr. K. Ross Toole, Hammond Professor of Western History, University of Montana; Tim M. Babcock, Governor; and the State Department of Public Instruction.

Illustrations on the preceding pages:
Cover photograph: Cowboys in Sandhills, Nebraska Department of Economic Development
Page 1: Commemorative stamps of historic interest
Pages 2-3: Glacier National Park, Travel Promotion Unit, Montana Department of Highways
Page 3: (Map) USDI Geological Survey
Pages 4-5: Bozeman area, EROS Space Photo, USDI Geological Survey, EROS Data Center

3 4 5 6 7 8 9 10 11 12 R 85 84 83 82 81 80

Project Editor, Revised Edition:
Joan Downing
Assistant Editor, Revised Edition:
Mary Reidy

Library of Congress Cataloging in Publication Data

Carpenter, John Allen, 1917-
Montana.

(His The new enchantment of America)
SUMMARY: A presentation of the Big Sky Country, including its history from the earliest times to the present, resources, famous citizens, and places of interest to visit.
1. Montana—Juvenile literature.
[1. Montana] I. Title. II. Series.
F731.3.C3 1979 978.6 79-683
ISBN 0-516-04126-6

Contents

Encampment of the Piegan Indians, *by Karl Bodmer. The Piegan were a division of the Blackfeet, the Indians who attacked John Colter and John Potts in 1808 in the Three Forks region.*

A Story to Set the Scene

RUN FOR YOUR LIFE!

"He had run half the distance when his strength began to fail and the blood to gush from his nostrils. At every leap the red stream spurted from him, and his limbs were growing rapidly weaker and weaker. He stopped and looked back; he had far outstripped (almost) all his pursuers and could get off if strength would only hold out. One solitary Indian, far ahead of the others, was rapidly approaching, with a spear in his right hand, and a blanket streaming behind from his left hand and shoulder."

As described by Thomas James, this was the critical point in a thrilling adventure story, and is one among many stories of the enchantment of Montana. Some of the quoted accounts may be exaggerated, but they convey a real sense of drama, and the basic facts are well known.

The exhausted runner was John Colter, at one time a member of the exploring party of Meriwether Lewis and William Clark.

In 1808 Colter came back to the region of the Three Forks of the Missouri River to hunt and trap with a man named John Potts.

Each man was paddling his own canoe in a small creek off the Jefferson River when a party of Blackfeet Indians suddenly appeared on the bank. Colter made a sign of peace and paddled to the shore, but Potts refused to come in, and was wounded with an arrow.

Then, according to James' account, ". . . he [Potts] levelled his rifle and shot an Indian dead. In an instant . . . Potts was made a riddle. . . . They dragged the body up onto the bank . . . and hacked it all to pieces and limb from limb."

Most of the Indians wanted to torture and kill Colter, too, but the chief asked Colter if he were a good runner. Colter was quite fast but pretended that he was very slow. They motioned him to go off a few hundred yards for a head start and then to begin running. They had already stripped him of all his clothes, and as he started to run, the prickly pear dug cruelly into his bare feet. Immediately the Indians began their pursuit.

The speed with which he ran for his life surprised even Colter, and he managed to outrun all the braves but one who followed him with a spear.

"Determined if possible to avoid the expected blow, he suddenly stopped, turned around, and spread out his arms," according to John Bradbury's account. "The Indian, surprised by the suddenness of the action, and perhaps at the bloody appearance of Colter (who had ruptured a blood vessel in his nose), also attempted to stop, but exhausted with running he [the Indian] fell whilst endeavouring to throw his spear, which stuck in the ground, and broke in his hand. Colter instantly snatched up the pointed part, with which he pinned him to the earth, and then continued his flight."

Staggering and almost dead from exhaustion, Colter reached the Madison River, five miles (eight kilometers) from his starting point.

"He plunged into the stream," as James continues the action, "and saw close beside him a beaver house. . . . Diving under the water he arose into the beaver house, where he found a dry and comfortable resting place. . . . The Indians soon came up, and in their search for him they stood upon the roof of his house of refuge, which he expected every moment to hear them breaking open. He also feared that they would set it on fire."

Most authorities say that the beaver house portion of the story is fiction. They claim that Colter was too large to get through the underground entrance of a beaver house and that he probably dived under a large pile of driftwood. However, James traveled in the same region with Colter two years later, and personally heard him describe his escape in vivid detail.

In any event, the Indians finally left; Colter came out at nightfall and began the long trip back to Manuel Lisa's fort at the mouth of the Big Horn River on the Yellowstone River.

There was a pass over the mountains, but "fearing that the Indians might have guarded this pass, which was the only outlet from the valley, and to avoid the danger of a surprise Colter . . . clambered up this fearful ascent. . . . " Later when he visited the spot with Colter, James wrote, "As I looked at its rugged and perpendicular sides I wondered how he ever reached the top."

Until he reached the open plains, Colter traveled at night, with only the blanket taken from the slain Indian to cover him from the bitter cold. He had only the roots of sheep sorrel to eat, and when he reached the fort eleven days after he started, he was "nearly exhausted by hunger, fatigue and excitement.... His beard was long, his face and whole body were thin and emaciated by hunger, and his limbs and feet swollen and sore. The company at the Fort did not recognize him in this dismal plight until he made himself known."

However, his strength and endurance were so great that before long he was on his way back to the Three Forks region to try to find his lost beaver traps. Once more he was attacked by the Indians, but as James relates, "he did escape once more, and was now *again* in the same country, courting the same dangers, which he had so often braved, and that seemed to have for him a kind of fascination.

"Such men, and there are thousands of such, can only live in a state of excitement and constant action. Perils and danger are their natural element, and their familiarity with them and indifference to their fate are well illustrated in these adventures of Colter."

Lay of the Land

"You have to push a lot of ground behind you to get places in this state" was the way one proud Montana man described the vast size of his state. He might have said simply that Montana is the fourth largest of all the states, with 147,138 square miles (381,086 square kilometers); about a third is made up of mountains and about two-thirds is plains.

Montana's lengthy northern boundary stretches along three Canadian provinces—British Columbia, Alberta, and Saskatchewan. The other boundaries touch four states—North Dakota and South Dakota on the east, Wyoming on the south, and Idaho on the west and southwest.

BIRTHPLACE OF RIVERS

The ragged southwest boundary is one of the few long irregular boundary lines in the country that does not follow a river. Part of this boundary runs parallel to the Continental Divide—where waters of the continent separate.

By a strange freak of geography a loop of the divide near the Yellowstone boundary runs in such a way that the eastbound waters begin their flow to the west, and the westbound waters begin their flow toward the east. This is probably the only sizable length of the divide where this is true.

About a fifth of Montana lies west of the Continental Divide. This part of the state is quite different in many ways, including its wildlife, plants, and climate.

There is another "divide" in Montana: portions of Glacier National Park and Teton County are on the northern side of the divide that sends waters to Hudson Bay by way of the Belly and St. Mary's rivers, then into the Saskatchewan River. The Missouri

Opposite: Glacier National Park

drainage system flows to the Mississippi River and finally to the Gulf of Mexico. Tributaries of the Columbia River in Montana flow to the Pacific Ocean. Montana is the only state with areas in all three drainage basins. The unique triple divide, from which water flows in all three directions, lies in Glacier National Park.

In addition to the Missouri, the major rivers of Montana are the Yellowstone, which flows into the Missouri just east of the Montana-North Dakota boundary, and the Clark Fork of the Columbia River, which receives the waters of the Blackfoot and Bitterroot rivers.

The Clark Fork, the main river of western Montana, was named for the famous explorer William Clark and it has many local names. It begins as Silver Bow Creek, then becomes the Deer Lodge River, changes to the Hellgate River, then the Missoula, and finally winds up as the Clark Fork. The Yellowstone River also has a fork named for Clark, Clark's Fork.

The Missouri River, the longest individual river in the country, has its source in Montana, where the Jefferson, Madison, and Gallatin rivers converge to form the mighty river. The place where they meet is known as the Three Forks. One account says that the Missouri takes its name from the tribe of Sioux Indians named Emessourita, whose name means "dwellers on the Big Muddy."

There is a strange similarity between the courses of the Missouri and the Mississippi. Contrary to expectation, both begin flowing north, then swing onto an eastward course, and finally turn south. The arc followed by the Missouri in these changes is vastly larger than that of the Mississippi, but the sequence of directions is identical. Both rivers even turn rather sharply again to the east as they near their mouths.

Other rivers include the Milk, an important northern tributary of the Missouri, Big Muddy, Poplar, Marias, Teton, Flathead, Rosebud, Tongue, Powder, Big Hole, Big Horn, and the famous Little Big Horn.

Other flowing waters include the many springs—both hot and cold. Giant Springs near Great Falls is claimed to be the world's largest; however, its daily flow of 388,800,000 gallons (almost 1,500,000 kiloliters) of water is less than half that of Big Springs in

East Rosebud Lake

Missouri. Where the crystal waters of Giant Springs enter the Missouri, the legendary muddy color of that river is cleared up for a long distance.

FROM HEAD (FLAT) TO TAIL (YELLOW)

Most of Montana's major lakes have been formed by damming the rivers. This system—designed for erosion and flood control, water conservation, and irrigation—includes twenty-four major dams.

Behind Fort Peck Dam, once the largest earthfill dam in the world, the Missouri has formed a huge reservoir, drowning 382.8 square miles (almost 1,000 square kilometers) of the Missouri Valley. Hungry Horse Dam is one of the world's largest concrete dams. At 525 feet (160 meters), Yellowtail Dam is the highest dam in the Missouri River basin. More than 1,400,000 cubic yards (1,070,000 cubic meters) of concrete were poured into it.

Flathead Lake, covering 189 square miles (490 square kilometers), is the largest natural lake in the state and one of the largest freshwater lakes west of the Mississippi.

Lake McDonald, 10 miles (16 kilometers) long, is the largest of the more than two hundred glacial lakes of Glacier National Park. McDonald is 437 feet (133 meters) deep in some places.

Nestled into the wild and ever-varied crevices, valley lowlands, and plains potholes are literally thousands of other lakes, reservoirs, and ponds. The total area of inland water in Montana is 1,402 square miles (3,631 square kilometers).

"LOS MONTANA"

Montana is the Spanish word for mountain. With a 200-mile-wide (320-kilometer) section across the state filled with range upon range of mountains, Montana lives up to its name. The first explorers called it the Land of the Shining Mountains.

When famed explorers Lewis and Clark came to Montana, Lewis wrote on May 26, 1805, "... on arriving to the summit [of] one of the highest points in the neighbourhood I thought myself well repaid for my labour; as from this point I beheld the Rocky Mountains for the first time ... these points of the Rocky Mountains were covered with snow and the sun shone on it in such manner as to give me the most plain and satisfactory view ... but when I reflected on the difficulties which this snowey barrier would most probably throw in my way to the Pacific, and the sufferings and hardships of myself and party in them, it in some measure counterballanced the joy I had felt in the first moments in which I gazed on them."

It is now thought that Lewis had confused the range known as the Little Rockies with the mightier range farther to the west.

Montana's highest peaks rise suddenly from the great plains in the Red Lodge region. Because there are few foothills in the area, the mountains appear much higher than their actual elevation. Included in this region are Granite Peak, 12,799 feet (3,901 meters), highest point in Montana, and Silver Run Peak, at 12,610 feet (3,843 meters) the second highest in the state.

The looming barrier of the Bitterroot Range covers the greatest area of any single range in Montana, forming a large part of the boundary with Idaho, which occupies the western slopes of those mountains.

Many of the numerous mountain ranges of the state have interesting and picturesque names, such as Bear's Paw and Beartooth mountains, the Sapphire Mountains, the Crazy Mountains, Swan and Elkhorn mountains, the Tobacco Root Mountains, Bridger and Mission ranges, Highwood Mountains, and the Pryors, part of the Big Horn Range. William Clark of the Lewis and Clark party named the Big Horn Mountains after killing two bighorn sheep in them.

Big Horn Canyon

IN ANCIENT TIMES

In a past too distant to imagine, much of the present state of Montana was formed under the waters of shallow seas. They came and went and laid unbelievably thick layers of gooey sediment that hardened into stone and can be seen in such places as the sides of Edwards Mountain, which are made up of this ancient hardened beach "mud." Later, some of the area raised slightly, providing a shoreline and coastal plain of a shallow, marshy arm of the great sea that covered America from the Gulf of Mexico to the Arctic Ocean.

"Next Dame Nature developed a gigantic stomach ache in western Montana," as Bob Fletcher describes it, "that caused her erstwhile placid countenance to crease with anguish. The largest wrinkles are the mountain ranges, the troughs between are structural valleys. The corrugations broadened and tapered off across eastern Montana into gently sloping anticlines."

In one of these awesome mountain-building operations known as the Lewis Overthrust, the Glacier Park area was lifted up and moved twenty-five miles (forty kilometers) across the plains to its present location.

The youngest mountains are the Beartooth Range—only about 75 million years of age, with a "recent" uplift that occurred not more than 1 million years ago. However, some of the rocks seen along Beartooth Highway are thought to be 2,700 million years old—among the oldest in the world.

Volcanic forces also shaped the land. In Bob Fletcher's picturesque description, "Hell boiled over in the west. Restless molten masses beneath the sedimentaries bulged and fractured them; volcanic ash deluged the valleys, and lava sheets flowed down the mountain sides. Central Montana broke out in a rash. Skin eruptions popped out like measles; the lava cores solidified and left the isolated mountain ranges of that section.

"The climate changed with the mountain building period and the dinosaurs quit cold. But there followed other warm intervals when monkeys, camels, sabre toothed tigers, and miniature three-toed horses romped over the landscape.

"Then the continental ice sheet slid down from west of Hudson Bay and covered all the northern part of the state east of the Rockies. It filled ancient stream beds with rock debris and started the ancient Missouri River cutting through new channels. When it receded a mere 30,000 years or so ago, it left its tracks in the shape of ridges or moraines. Since then the changes in Montana's surface have been through the less spectacular agencies of erosion."

Of the four separate ice sheets that crunched into the region, the last—known as the Wisconsin—was at least 10,000 feet (3,050 meters) thick—almost 2 miles (3.2 kilometers)! Most of the natural lakes in present Montana were created when piles of dirt called moraines backed up the rivers with natural dams.

Sixty relatively small glaciers now occupy parts of Glacier National Park, but these were formed later and are not descendants of the ancient glaciers, from which the park takes its name. Because of the general warming trend of the climate, it is felt that in time these glaciers will disappear; they have been receding for some time.

"BURIAL PLACE OF MONSTERS"

The Yellowstone Valley, said Addison Quivey in 1874, is "valuable for neither agriculture, grazing, nor minerals, but . . . interesting . . . as the last home and burial place of the horrible monsters of the earliest animal creation."

Today's residents have a much higher opinion of the valley, but they agree with Quivey about the "monsters." Montana is one of the richest regions anywhere for fossils, the remains of those monsters and other creatures not so monstrous.

One of the most complete dinosaur specimens ever unearthed was found north of Jordan on Hell Creek; this was the fierce tyrannosaurus rex, king of the dinosaurs. A very complete skeleton of a triceratops, a dinosaur with a three-foot (one-meter) horn over each eye and another on his nose, was found near Glendive. Other dinosaur remains have been found and portions of dinosaur eggs were picked up near Red Lodge.

Not far from Billings a rare hoplitosaurus was found, a relative of the horned toad, except it was 15 feet (4.6 meters) tall.

A most unusual fossil was that of one of the oldest known primates—a relative of present-day monkey, ape, and man.

Remains of a giant sequoia and other petrified trees were found at the fossil beds near Baker. Other well-known Montana fossil sources are Hysham, Ekalaka, Little Dry Creek, Fort Peck, and Harlowtown.

"A VERY EXTRAORDINARY CLIMATE TO BEHOLD"

Montana people are said to "take the climate without undue complaint. . . . There isn't a month in Montana without at least one day in which a man will be comfortable in his shirt sleeves. Ever feel a chinook? Chinook? It's a warm wind from the west. Last time it started up, a rancher who'd come to town by sled just managed, going home, to keep his front bobs on the snow. Like to killed his horse doing it."

The exaggeration is not extreme. Balmy days do come in midwinter. A temperature variation of seventy degrees Fahrenheit (thirty-nine degrees Celsius) in a few hours is not unusual.

Explorer William Clark commented about Montana snow in his notes for May 2, 1805: ". . . the snow which fell to day was about 1 in deep, a verry extraodernarey climate to behold the trees Green & flowers spred on the plain, & Snow an inch deep." Snow rarely stays on the ground very long except at high altitudes.

Precipitation in Montana is scanty, averaging about 15 inches (38 centimeters) per year. Rain sometimes falls in an extremely limited area, as evidenced by the fanciful tale of the farmer who saw a storm coming up behind him; he urged his horses on as fast as they could go and reached home without getting wet, but he looked around only to find the wagon box full of rainwater.

Footsteps on the Land

EARLIEST LANDLORDS

Life in prehistoric Montana has been divided into three periods—Ancient Hunters, Middle Period, and Late Period, ending about a thousand years ago.

Some of the oldest evidence of human occupation is found in caves near Billings—probably eight to twelve thousand years old. The ancient hunters followed the herds of big game animals, killing them with *atlatls*—javelinlike throwing sticks with carefully made stone spear points.

In the Middle Period the plains' climate became hot and dry. Herds of giant game animals disappeared. Hunters had to turn to the smaller animals such as antelope and rabbits. Women searched for edible roots to add to the diet. Spear points were not so finely made as they had been earlier. These people left behind them many items of daily use, including some slabs for grinding seeds into flour and lined pits for baking camus and other roots.

With the coming of more moisture, buffalo returned to the plains, and the wealth of meat, bones, and skins attracted more people to the region. The bow and arrow became known, and a very efficient kind of buffalo hunt was devised. A carefully planned drive stampeded an entire herd over a cliff or into a bog or corral, such as a natural ravine, or into a crude structure of stones or logs.

THE INDIANS

In the 1600s the plains Indians received a wonderful gift, the horse, from the Spanish. Indians of the south stole as many horses as they could. As the numbers of Indian horses grew, the southern Indians traded with those to the north, and by 1700 horses were owned by Indians as far north as present-day Canada.

The horse changed the Indians' entire way of life, providing a means of fast travel, new types of warfare, a carrier for burdens, and

Buffalo Dance of the Mandan, *by Karl Bodmer. The buffalo hunt was one of the most important events in the life of plains Indians.*

even a means of demonstrating bravery. To the Indian, stealing a horse was one of the bravest and most daring feats possible. This attitude later brought about much misunderstanding with the settlers.

The plains Indians soon became complete masters of the horse, ranking among the greatest horsemen of the world.

The more permanent homes of the Indians were lodges of skins and mud over frameworks of sticks or poles. The light skin tepee, sometimes used as a permanent home, was also used as a temporary dwelling, especially when the Indians were traveling.

Many tribes placed their dead in trees, and trees frequently were seen with grisly "decorations" of skulls and bones.

The buffalo hunt was one of the most important events in the life of plains Indians. Meriwether Lewis wrote: "Today we passed on the Sard. [starboard] side the remains of . . . many mangled carcases of Buffalow which had been driven over a precipice of 120 feet by the Indians and perished . . . there remained the fragments of at least a hundred carcases they created a most horrid stench. In this manner the Indians of the Missouri distroy vast herds of buffaloe at a stroke."

He went on to tell how one of the Indian men would disguise himself with a buffalo robe and head, and decoy the buffalo over the cliff as the other tribesmen shouted and yelled to drive them on.

Almost every portion of the buffalo was used—skin for robes and clothing; horns for bows, cups, spoons, and platters; and the meat, both fresh and dried. Dried meat was known as pemmican, a kind of sausage made of the cured meat mixed with chokecherries or other berries. The Musselshell River was known as the Dried Meat River because of the quantity of pemmican made on its banks.

The largest tribes of the plains were the Crow and Blackfeet.

The Crow, or Absarokee ("people of the raven"), may have originated as far south as Mexico. The Crow had a strong feeling for the land, expressed by one of them named Curly when he said: "The soil you see is not ordinary soil—it is the dust of the blood, the flesh, and bones of our ancestors. You will have to dig down to find Nature's earth, for the upper portion is Crow, my blood and my dead. I do not want to give it up."

The wide-ranging Blackfeet were feared as warriors; as one writer put it, "no tribe ever exceeded them in bravery." Their major divisions were Pikuni or Piegan, Blood, and the main Blackfeet tribe, all related to the Algonquin nation. Legend says that the Blackfeet got the name when the Sun god gave one of them a black dye to stain his feet, making him fast enough to run down the swiftest game.

Cheyenne were also of the Algonquin nation, as were the Arapaho. The Shoshone hunted in an area from the Big Horn Mountains to the ranges of the Pacific Coast. The Assiniboin, called the Mountain Sioux, were known to be generally friendly with the settlers.

Other Blackfeet divisions included the Minnetaree (Gros Ventres of the River), and Atsina (Gros Ventres of the Mountains), who used the dialect of the Arapaho.

The Confederated Tribes of Flathead included the Salish, Kalispel, and the Kootenai tribes. One of the most interesting Indian beliefs is that held by the Salish, who considered that the beavers were bad Indians, condemned to the form of a beast and constant hard work because of evil in their former lives.

One of the least-known and peaceful tribes was the Sheepeater, or Arrowmaker, found in the Yellowstone Park area where other Indians were afraid to live. The Sheepeater were noted for their beautiful arrowheads chipped from obsidian (natural volcanic glass) of the region.

THE INTREPID ONES

Montana history pulses with action and contains many notable characters. Few were more interesting than the dauntless early explorers.

In 1742 two brothers named Verendrye made their way over the Great Plains from Canada, across the Dakotas, and entered Montana at the southeast. On New Year's Day 1743, they shielded their eyes from the sun and marveled at the beauty of the "shining mountains" they saw, but we do not know exactly which mountains. Francis and Louis Verendrye are the first Europeans known to have set foot in what is now Montana, which has been known as the Land of the Shining Mountains ever since.

The Yellowstone River had been named by James Mackay as early as 1795, and there undoubtedly had been French trappers and explorers in the area, but little was known about the region when it came under under United States' control as part of the vast Louisiana Purchase in 1803. This included all of present-day Montana up to the Great Divide.

To find out about the region, President Thomas Jefferson sent out a group of men who have since become known as the greatest exploring party in American history. Led by Meriwether Lewis and William Clark, this party spent more than two years in an unknown wilderness, facing hostile Indians and some of the fiercest animals of the continent, and lost only one man on the whole trip. His death was due to natural causes.

After spending the winter of 1804-1805 at the Mandan Indian village in North Dakota, Lewis and Clark pushed on and entered Montana where the Missouri River cuts the boundary line just west of the mouth of the great Yellowstone River, where they arrived on April 26, 1805. On this leg of the trip and on the homeward journey, the expedition covered more territory in what is now Montana than in any other state—a total of 1,940 miles (3,122 kilometers).

"AN ESSENTIAL POINT IN GEOGRAPHY"

As he looked proudly at his boats, Captain Lewis could not help remarking in his journal, "This little fleet, altho' not quite so rispectable as those of Columbus or Capt. Cook, were still viewed by us with as much pleasure as those deservedly famed adventurers ever beheld theirs; and I dare say with quite as much anxiety for their safety and preservation. We were now about to penetrate a country at least two thousand miles in width, on which the foot of civilized man had never trodden . . . and these little vessells contained every article by which we were to expect to subsist or defend ourselves."

Both Lewis and Clark kept remarkably complete journals, leaving an unequaled record of the country and everything in it, as well as giving later readers a sense of awe at their bravery.

On May 8 they discovered the Milk River and on May 20 came to the Musselshell. Clark named the Judith River for a woman he had left behind in Virginia. Then on June 3 they came to still another river.

"The whole of my party to a man," Lewis wrote, "were fully persuaded that this river was the Missouri, but being fully of the opinion that it was neither the main stream, nor that which it would be advisable for us to take, I determined to give it a name and in honour of Miss Maria W--d [his cousin, Maria Wood] called it Marias River."

Choosing which of these rivers to take was the most important problem the party had yet faced. "To ascend such a stream to the rocky Mountains or perhaps much further before we could inform ourselves whether it did approach the Columbia or not, and then be obligated to return and take the other stream would not only loose us the whole of this season but would probably so dishearten the party that it might defeat the expedition altogether."

They went up both streams for some way trying to obtain some clue, and Lewis finally persuaded Clark that he was right. Although the other men still felt that Marias River was the Missouri, they followed Lewis up the other branch, and his judgment was rewarded when they came to the most notable landmark on the river, which the Indians of North Dakota had told them they would find.

Lewis described it: "My ears were saluted with the agreeable sound of a fall of water and advancing a little further I saw the spray arrise above the plain . . . which soon began to make a roaring too tremendious to be mistaken for any cause short of the great falls of the Missouri . . . the grandest sight I ever beheld."

They had to spend a month portaging their boats and supplies around the Great Falls, then pressed on toward an even greater discovery—the still unknown source of the mighty Missouri River.

On July 25, Clark wrote matter-of-factly about one of the most dramatic geographical discoveries of the country: "a fine morning . . . we proceeded on a few miles to the three forks of the Missouri . . . those three forks are nearly of a Size, the North fork appears to have the most water and must be Considered as the one best calculated for us to ascend."

Lewis continued: "Believing this to be an essential point in the geography of this western part of the Continent I determined to remain at all events untill I obtained the necessary data for fixing it's latitude Longitude &c . . . I walked down to the middle fork and examined and compared it with the S.W. fork but could not satisfy myself which was the largest stream of the two, in fact they appeared as if they had been cast in the same mould there being no difference in character or size, therefore to call either of these streams the Missouri would be giving it a preference which it's size does not warrant as it is not larger than the other."

And so Lewis decided on a fact with which later geographers agreed. The place where the three rivers came together was the birthplace of the Missouri River, and the three streams which united to form it were only tributaries.

Meriwether Lewis and William Clark, leading the most famous expedition in American history, spent more than two years on a round-trip exploration of the continent from St. Louis, Missouri, to the Pacific Ocean. The party came upon the Great Falls of the Missouri River (below) in June 1805.

Pompey's Pillar, a landmark on the Lewis and Clark Trail, was named for Pomp, the young son of Sacajawea, the expedition's Indian guide.

ON THE CREST OF THE CONTINENT

Lewis went on to say that they "agreed to name them [the three rivers] after the President of the United States and the Secretaries of the Treasury and State, having previously named one river in honour of the Secretaries of War and Navy. . . . We called the S.W. fork, that which we meant to ascend, Jefferson's River in honor of that illustrious personage Thomas Jefferson (the author of our enterprize) the Middle fork we called Madison's River in honor of James Madison and the S.E. Fork we called Gallitin's River in honor of Albert Gallitin [Gallatin]."

They went on up the Jefferson River to its forks, which they named Philosophy, Wisdom, and Philanthropy in honor of President Jefferson's "cardinal virtues." These rivers have since been given new names, such as the Big Hole in place of the Wisdom.

At last the expedition reached the highest point on the farthest reaches of the Missouri and its tributaries—known to geographers as the "ultimate source of the Missouri." Lewis called it "the most distant fountain of the waters of the Mighty Missouri in surch of which we have spent so many toilsome days and wristless nights. . . . Two miles below McNeal [one of his men] had exultingly stood with a foot on each side of this little rivulet and thanked his god that he had lived to bestride the mighty & heretofore deemed endless Missouri."

A short time later Lewis wrote: "I now decended the mountain about ¾ of a mile to a handsome bold running Creek of cold Clear water. Here I first tasted the water of the great Columbia river." Lewis had become the first American explorer of record to stand on this portion of the great Continental Divide, and for the first time he was on the western slopes of the mountains where the waters ran to the Pacific. This is now called Lemhi Pass.

THEIR KINGDOM FOR A HORSE

Some time before this the rivers had become too shallow for boats, which the party had hidden. Now it was necessary to meet the Indians of the region and trade for horses—the expedition now had to carry its supplies over the mountains. Surprisingly, they had not seen a single Indian since they had left the Mandan villages of North Dakota.

In what is now Idaho, Lewis finally found a party of Indians and after much discussion brought the chief and some of his tribe back over the mountains to meet Clark and the rest of his party. There they traded for horses and soon the men left Montana on their long, perilous way to the Pacific Ocean.

On the way home they again entered Montana, on June 29, 1806; at the place they called Traveller's Rest, the party divided. Lewis went north down the Bitterroot River and crossed the Continental Divide on July 7, 1806, at what is called Lewis and Clark Pass. Later the party traveled down Marias River. On this part of the trip the first hostile Indians were encountered. Two Blackfeet Indians were killed in the ensuing conflict.

Clark crossed the Continental Divide at Gibbon's Pass, and with ten men he started up the Gallatin, passed over a buffalo trail, and found the Yellowstone River, near the present town of Livingston. Indians stole the party's horses, and the group had to go down the river in crafts known as bull boats. By August 12 the entire expedition was reunited, and September 23, 1806, found them back in St. Louis.

MASTERY OF THE MOUNTAIN MEN

Even before Lewis and Clark reached Montana, the trading party of François Antoine Larocque had gone overland to reach the point where the Big Horn River meets the Yellowstone River. Then the men traveled down the Yellowstone doing some trading with the Indians for the North West Company.

Businessman Manuel Lisa heard the Lewis and Clark accounts of the rich fur country of the West. In 1807 Lisa took forty-two men with him to build a trading fort on the Yellowstone River at the Big Horn's mouth. This was the first trading station in Montana.

The greatest geographer of his day in the Americas, David Thompson, built the first European-type house in Montana, near what is now Thompson Falls. He also was employed by the North West Company.

A trading post was built in 1810 close to the Three Forks by Pierre Menard and Andrew Henry, but twenty men were killed in attacks by the Blackfeet, and the post was abandoned. Beginning in 1822 the company of William H. Ashley had many men in the upper Missouri region trapping and trading for furs. John Jacob Astor's American Fur Company operated probably the largest chain of fur posts, built under the direction of Kenneth McKenzie, the company's regional manager. The posts included Fort Union near the mouth of the Yellowstone, and Forts Chardon, Benton, Lewis, Cass, Van Buren, Piegan, and McKenzie.

Traders or mountain men who braved the perils of the trail, weather, and Indian attack had in their number some of the most famous men of the early West—Jim Bridger, John Colter, Major Andrew Henry, Hugh Glass, and many others. They had an extraordinary knowledge of the wilderness and its ways. It was said that a mountain man could hastily draw a chart on buckskin with a piece of charcoal and it would guide one safely to any destination in the almost trackless wastes.

The fur trapping and trading period lasted roughly from 1807 to 1843, with the beaver the main commodity. In many places the valuable fur animals had been trapped almost to extinction. Beaver

This William Henry Jackson watercolor shows the 1824 fur traders' annual rendezvous, at which traders and trappers exchanged furs and supplies.

hats eventually went out of fashion, and the trapping-trading period came to a close.

Famous visitors in the region during the period included Prince Maximilian, of a German family; George Catlin, famed painter of the Indians; and John James Audubon, the noted naturalist painter of birds.

NEW ENDEAVORS

About this time, the great rush to the West was beginning. Travelers on the Oregon Trail, and later the California gold rush adventurers, passed to the south of Montana. Soon there was little grazing along the travel routes for the ox teams that hauled the prairie schooners and wagons. Poorly fed, hard-worked steers collapsed and were abandoned. Many mountain men went south to pick up abandoned strays and bring them back to Montana. There the wonderful grasses soon had the animals back in good condition. In a few months the cattle could be taken back to the trails and traded to eager travelers one for two; then the process was repeated with the new animals.

One of the greatest disasters ever to strike the Indians was the smallpox epidemic of 1837, deliberately brought to the area by pioneer traders by means of infected blankets. About half the Indians of the region lost their lives. Sacrifice Cliff, which rises 200 feet (61 meters) above the Yelowstone River near Billings, takes its name from the fact that a number of Indians rode their horses over the cliff to their deaths in an effort to appease the gods and bring the smallpox to a halt.

Missionary work among the Indians began when one of America's most noted missionary-explorers, Father Pierre Jean De Smet, founded St. Mary's Mission in 1841. Stevensville, called the first permanent settlement in Montana, came into being nearby. The second mission in the state was St. Ignatius, founded in 1854.

The first steamboat reached Fort Union in 1832. The first crop was planted in the Bitterroot Valley in 1842. Fort Lewis was built in 1842 at the point where the Missouri River could no longer be navigated by boats; in 1847 Fort Connah near St. Ignatius was the last of the Hudson's Bay Company's forts to be established in what is now the United States. The Mullan Road, eventually running 624 miles (1,004 kilometers) between Fort Benton and Walla Walla, Washington, was begun in 1858 by John Mullan; eventually it became the first road for wagons over the northern Rockies.

By the mid-1850s some numbers of the backwash from the California goldfields had begun to find their way into Montana, joining the cattle-trading camps and doing some prospecting.

Even with these newcomers there was in all the vast present state only a small non-native population. However, the stage was set for interesting and explosive developments.

Yesterday and Today

WEALTH! EUREKA!

Father De Smet, pioneer missionary to the Indians, knew a secret that might well have cost him his life, but he never told it. He had probably known for years that there was gold in the Montana region, but he refused to reveal this because he thought the rush of gold seekers would be disastrous for the Indians.

As early as 1852 François Finlay (also known as Benetsee) had found gold near present-day Goldcreek, but nothing much came of it. A gold discovery by the Stuarts actually started the state's mining industry in 1857-1858. These discoveries brought in men from other gold fields, and in July, 1862, John White made Montana's first substantial discovery on Grasshopper Creek. The camp of Bannack came into existence and within a few days it had a population of more than five hundred—Montana's first town!

For about a year Bannack reigned supreme as the only important gold center east of the Continental Divide. Then six miners under the leadership of Bill Fairweather began a search for gold. The events of May 26, 1863, were retold by Henry Edgar, one of the group: "We crossed the Madison and came up . . . Wigwam Gulch, camped beside a lake at the foot of Bald Mountain. . . . The other four proceeded up the gulch . . . prospecting. About sundown Bill went across the creek to picket the horses.

" 'There is a piece of bedrock projecting,' said Bill, 'and we had better go over and see if we cannot get enough money to buy a little tobacco.' So Bill took the pick and shovel and I took a pan and we crossed the creek. He dug the dirt up and shoveled it into the pan. I went down the creek to wash it. While I was washing the dirt, he scratched around in the bedrock with his butcher knife [and] called: 'I've found a scad!'

"I had the pan about half washed down, and I replied: 'If you have one I have a thousand.' And so I had."

They named the place Alder Gulch, "on account of the heavy clump of alders along the . . . creek," but they could not keep their find a secret; in less than a week swarms of eager gold seekers were scouring the gulch. The community was organized and given the name Varina by Confederate sympathizers (the Civil War was then raging), in honor of the wife of Jefferson Davis, president of the Confederacy. The town judge, a Union partisan, refused to issue the necessary papers for this name, and he called it Virginia City—the first town to be incorporated in Montana. It has been labeled the "cradle of Montana." Within a year after the discovery, it was estimated that ten thousand people were living within a ten-mile (sixteen-kilometer) radius of the discovery point.

Later in 1863, John M. Bozeman made a road from the Oregon Trail to the mining camps and brought in a large group in 1864. Jim Bridger also began to guide groups into the area. Almost at once the Indians started attacking travelers on the trail because the people were coming onto Indian land in violation of the Indians' treaty rights.

On May 26, 1864, Congress created the Montana territory, with Bannack as the first capital and Sidney Edgerton as first governor. Over the years, Montana had been a part of the territories of Oregon, Washington, Nebraska, Dakota, and Idaho. The story is told that four brothers were all born in the same house near present-day Frenchtown, but each had been a native of a different territory. Now at last the people would have a government of their own and not have to travel to some far-off capital.

July 14, 1864, marked the beginning of another gold stampede, exceeding any of the others. A party of four headed by John Cowan had been unlucky at Virginia City; they tried other places without success. Discouraged and out of funds, they were about to give up when one of the party insisted that they try just once more in a small gulch. They agreed. "This little gulch on the Prickly Pear is our last chance." When they made their strike there, they called the place Last Chance Gulch. Today the main street of Helena runs down Last Chance Gulch.

The many visitors to Elkhorn, a Montana ghost town (opposite), are stirred by echoes of an exciting past.

Panners today still find a little gold.

The city received its name when the settlers who rushed to the place decided the name Last Chance was not dignified enough and accepted John Somerville's suggestion of Helena, in honor of his home town in Minnesota.

Butte got its start as a gold camp in 1864 and many other camps and mines sprang up. At Yellowstone City the miners spent the first winter living in holes in the ground. One amateur miner asked an old-timer where he should commence his digging. He pointed out the worst-looking spot he could find; on that spot the novice struck one of the richest small areas ever found, which he called Montana Bar. Silver Bow Creek, Lewison, Marysville, and many others became noted for their riches. One observer remarked sarcastically, "Out there every prairie dog hole is a gold mine; every hill a mountain; every creek a river, and everybody you meet is a liar." There may have been exaggeration, but the wealth that poured out of Montana mines was real enough.

At Bannack, the territory's first legislature held its meeting in a log cabin, but soon the capital was moved to more prosperous Virginia City, 55 miles (89 kilometers) away. Even at this time there was a move for statehood; a convention called by acting Governor General Thomas Francis Meagher drafted a constitution that had to be sent as far as St. Louis for printing. Before it reached that city the constitution was lost, and was never recovered.

Even more mysterious was the disappearance of Governor Meagher himself. On July 1, 1867, Meagher, a Civil War hero, reached Fort Benton where he expected to take a steamboat to continue a trip. He went to his steamboat stateroom and was never seen again. It was said that political enemies had done away with him, but his true fate remains a mystery.

ROAD TO THE GALLOWS

The wildness of the stampede to the riches of Montana was similar to many others. It brought the usual greenhorns and gamblers, merchants and lawless characters, as well as miners and prospectors. The government was so new and distances so great that the laws could not be enforced. As someone has remarked, "There was a saloon entrance every forty feet and a bad man on every corner."

One band of desperate outlaws terrorized the district for months, robbing the stagecoaches of gold consignments and murdering at least a hundred persons. At last the citizens organized as vigilantes. As the bandits were captured and hung, the details of the leadership came to light. Bannack was horrified that the man it had elected sheriff, "genial" Henry Plummer, was the leader of the outlaws. He had created an efficient crime organization. Plummer met the same fate as twenty-eight other members of his gang—hanging.

Burials were often quick and informal in the "Boothills" of the time. A favorite pastime of the gravediggers was to see who could toss the most pennies between the cracks of the hastily nailed coffins. On one grave the crutches of a crippled man were used as his tombstone.

As time went on, of course, law and order became increasingly effective, but as late as 1883 a territorial governor had to wire the postmaster general in Washington: "Vigilantes at Greenhorn, Montana, have removed postmaster by hanging . . . Office now vacant."

"A GREAT CHIEF; MY PEOPLE DID NOT WANT HIS SCALP"

The Indians were a far greater peril than outlaws. Eastern Montana was part of an area set aside by treaty for the Indians, especially the Sioux. Non-Indians were technically forbidden to enter it. Western Montana had become a "settled" land, while the east was still held by the Indians. The Indians were not content to sit back and watch as more and more people violated this treaty, and the government seemed unable to do anything about it. It was obvious that the Indians' way of life was being forced from them by either deceit or treaty.

Although in 1868 "impregnable" Fort Benton, defended by only eleven soldiers, had stood off an attack of Sioux, the government felt forced to honor its treaty and closed the forts and shut off the Bozeman Trail to further travel.

The pressure to open up the area became so great, however, that the United States finally decided to make new treaties with the Indians and to place them on reservations. In a last desperate attempt to save their land and traditional manner of living, the Indians went on the offensive. All across the Western plains some of the Indian leaders organized their forces and attacked again and again.

This warfare reached its peak in what is probably the best-known battle ever to take place between Indians and United States government troops. On June 25, 1876, Lieutenant Colonel George

Armstrong Custer (a major general in the Civil War) and five troops of the Seventh United States Cavalry were completely destroyed by Sioux and Cheyenne Indians at the Little Big Horn River, south and east of Hardin. Only one horse remained alive of all the government men and animals.

Not far away, Major Marcus A. Reno and three units were involved in heavy fighting. Although their losses were severe, they were not wiped out.

Because no one of Custer's forces survived, the details of the battle have never become known. Exactly what happened is one of the great mysteries of American history.

Frederic Remington's painting of Custer's Last Stand.

Among the many puzzles are such questions as why Custer split his forces into four parts. How did the Indians get the advanced Winchester rifles, much better than the guns of Custer's men? Why did Custer rush into battle so swiftly? Why didn't the forces of Fred W. Benteen hurry to his aid?

Sitting Bull, who was a medicine man, not a chief, was not present at the battle he is so often credited with winning. His Sioux associates told him about the battle, and talking with a *New York Herald* reporter he later gave his version of the fight:

"Hah! A great white chief whom I met once spoke these words, 'silver aspens,' trees that shake; these were the Long Hair's [Custer's] soldiers. They did not tremble because they were afraid, but because they were tired. They were too tired. These men who came with Long Hair were as good men as ever fought. When they rode up, their horses were tired, and they were tired. When they got off from their horses they could not stand firmly on their feet. They swayed to and fro—so my young men have told me—like the limbs of cypresses in a great wind. Some of them staggered under the weight of their guns.

"But they began to fight at once. By this time our camps were aroused, and there were plenty of warriors to meet them. They fired with needle guns. We replied with magazine guns—repeating rifles. Our young men rained lead across the river and drove the white braves back [referring perhaps to the action against Reno].

"The trouble with the soldiers was they were so exhausted and their horses bothered them so much they could not take good aim. Some of their horses broke away from them and left them to stand and drop and die. When Long Hair, the general, found that he was so outnumbered and threatened on his flanks, he took the best course he could have taken. The bugle blew. It was an order to fall back. All the men fell back fighting and dropping. They could not fire fast enough, though. But from our side it was so [Sitting Bull clapped his hands to indicate the rapidity of the Indian firing]. They could not stand up under such fire.

"They kept in pretty good order. They would fall back across a coulee and make a fresh stand on higher ground. There was one part driven out there [pointing to a map], and there a great many men were killed. Every man kept fighting to the last. There were no cowards on either side.

"None of them died on horseback. . . . One by one the officers fell. . . . The Long Hair stood like a sheaf of corn with all the ears fallen around him.

"A few stood by him. He killed a man when he fell. He laughed. He had fired his last shot. He rose up on his hands and tried another shot, but his pistol would not go off. One other man was kneeling, but that was all; he died before Long Hair.

"Long Hair was not scalped. He was a great chief. My people did not want his scalp."

Later, General Nelson A. Miles defeated Sitting Bull at the Tongue River's mouth and at Cedar Creek. This was followed by a defeat of Chief Crazy Horse near Birney. The Indian threat finally was ended in battles in other states.

DEFEAT OF AN INDIAN GENIUS

An entirely different kind of Indian "disturbance" came to Montana in 1877. The government had been trying to force the Nez Percé to leave their ancestral lands and go to remote reservations. With their famous tribal guardian, Chief Joseph, the Nez Percé decided to flee to Canada and ask for asylum there. All of Joseph's followers—including women, children, and old men—left their homes in eastern Oregon, Washington, and western Idaho, pursued by government troops.

The masterly retreat over 1,600 miles (2,575 kilometers) of three states, hampered by all their belongings and their women and children, is one of the epic marches of history. Until this disturbance, the Nez Percé had never warred with the settlers, and on their march Chief Joseph insisted that they inflict as little harm as possible.

With little conflict they crossed Idaho, entered Montana, and camped on Big Hole prairie, August 7, 1877. On August 9, United

Montana artist Bob Scriver's diorama (above) shows the embattled Chief Joseph of the Nez Percé talking to his people at the Battle of the Bear's Paw. The painting below shows him walking slowly toward the assembled cavalry officers to accept the terms of surrender offered to him in 1877.

States forces under John Gibbon made a surprise attack on the camp and almost succeeded in capturing it, but the Indians drove them off under the brilliant leadership of their war chief, Looking Glass.

Leaving a rear guard, the Indians hurried into retreat and escaped into the Yellowstone Park region, embittered by this experience and the losses of their loved ones. They then moved north again and through Montana, showing remarkable endurance. Only a few miles before reaching Canada, they made camp, thinking they had crossed the border. The weary band again was surprised by a force under Nelson A. Miles, in what is now known as the Battle of the Bear's Paw, near Bear's Paw Mountain.

The Nez Percé were still able to resist, and Miles prepared for a siege. After six days of attack, Joseph sent out this pathetic word: "Our chiefs are dead; the little children are freezing. My people have no blankets, no food. From where the sun now stands, I will fight no more, forever." He later explained, "My people needed rest—we wanted peace."

Joseph and his warriors might have escaped if they had abandoned their women, children, and wounded. They refused to do this.

Colonel Miles admired the courage of the Nez Percé and promised them safe return to Idaho. But the government did not honor this promise.

The Battle of the Bear's Paw, in August 1877, was the last large-scale Indian fighting in Montana.

GROWTH AND CHANGE

In 1866 the first cattle were driven over the long hard trail from Texas to Montana. From that time on, the cattle industry grew until it reached its peak in the 1880s and 1890s, although the awful winter of 1886-1887 wiped out many outfits completely and it took years to rebuild the herds.

On July 5, 1881, the Northern Pacific Railroad crossed the eastern boundary of Montana at Glendive. The last spike was driven in with great ceremony at Goldcreek near Garrison in 1883. At last the almost endless length of the state was served by gleaming rails.

The beginning of agriculture, which has since grown tremendously, came in 1882 with the first irrigation in Montana.

In 1884 the people approved a constitution which they hoped would create a state. Congress took five years to give an answer, then required a new constitution, which was drawn up. It included the entire Magna Carta, Declaration of Independence, Articles of Confederation, United States Constitution, and the organic and enabling acts of the territory. Weighed down, possibly, by this massive show of constitutional law, Congress approved, and Montana became a state on November 8, 1889.

More and more people were coming to find homesites where they could farm the land. On the open prairies often the only building material was the ground itself. Strips of sod were cut out and laid like bricks to make walls. In the spring a traveler who spotted a mound on the prairie covered with spring blooms of all kinds might be quite sure he was approaching a farmer's sod house. Others used the mud to cast adobe bricks, which were dried in the sun and provided material to erect durable homes.

The cattlemen, whose herds had roamed the range, foresaw great damage to their business if the increasing numbers of farmers continued to fence off the land. Clashes between farmers and cattlemen were sharp and frequent, but the farmers generally won in the end.

Farms and fences also doomed the way of life of many cowboys, who rode, roped, branded, herded, slept on the ground, kept watch much of the night, had a frantic time overcoming stampedes—and were paid thirty dollars a month for all this. Yet most of them appeared to like the life. When the fences came, they might lament: "I've hung up the saddle and turned out ol' Buck; I'm feelin' right solemn and blue. I'm a bowlegged puncher who's shore outa luck, and I reckon my punchin' is through. It don't matter which way I heads in the morn, I'm shore to fetch up at a fence. . . . So my mind is made up and my purpose is grim, and I blush at the thought of my shame . . . that Montana Slim has to play such a card in the game. I can't back out now . . . for I just bought a rake and a second-hand plow."

In addition to the cattlemen's feuds with farmers, the cattle interests also fought the coming of sheep, and there were such occurrences as the 1901 killing of two thousand sheep by masked men at Lame Deer.

President Theodore Roosevelt came to Gardiner in 1903 to lay the cornerstone of the Roosevelt Arch over the northern entrance to Yellowstone Park. The state flag approved in 1905 was the same flag carried by the First Montana Infantry regiment in the Philippines during the Spanish-American War.

Montana made national history when in 1917 Jeannette Rankin of Missoula took her seat as the first woman ever elected to the United States House of Representatives. A dramatic scene in that body's long life occurred when the congressmen were casting their votes for United States' entry into World War I.

At first Jeannette Rankin passed; then Congressman Cannon said, "You cannot afford not to vote. You represent the womanhood of the country in the American Congress." She stood and said, "I want to stand by my country, but I cannot vote for war. . . . I vote No." She sank into her seat and began to cry. She received both praise and criticism for her action. She repeated this stand on the vote for World War II.

The 1920s saw such different happenings as the building of many fine roads, the discovery of oil, the much-publicized heavyweight title fight at Shelby between Jack Dempsey and Tommy Gibbons (which turned out to be a flop), and the uncovering of the Teapot Dome oil scandal through the work of Montana Senators Burton K. Wheeler and Thomas J. Walsh.

Glacier National Park was rededicated in 1932 in cooperation with Canada, as the American part of the International Peace Park, symbolizing the long, peaceful relations between the two peoples. The Going-to-the-Sun Highway was completed across the park in 1933, and mighty Fort Peck Dam was begun in that same year.

These pleasant events of the 1930s were offset by bitter problems and disasters. A series of earthquakes shook the state beginning in 1935. Nature was even more severe with Montana in the worst drought in the country's history. The powder-dry soil was picked up by the winds, and to the disaster of the drought was added the awful effects of the worst dust storms ever to plague the United States. Many were forced to abandon their lands. Once-pleasant houses stood empty and windowless on the parched land. The Great Depression ruined hundreds more in both the rural areas and the cities. By 1938 almost all of the mines in Butte had closed.

Gradually, however, the rains came again; trees were planted and other measures were taken against the dust storms. Government work projects gave employment to many and brought in money to help the economy.

On August 17, 1959, the people of Montana were given a sharp reminder that the earth's surface is still changing. A spectacularly scenic area of Montana suddenly was rocked by a severe earthquake, making the state the focus of world attention. As the ground

George Catlin's painting of a Mandan Indian village shows a vanished way of life.

rumbled and shifted, buckled and twisted, great crevices opened up and sections of highway disappeared; suddenly a whole mountainside collapsed into the Madison River, and a new lake—Quake Lake—was born.

Montana became the site of one of the most important of the world's military installations, when the nation's largest intercontinental ballistics missile complex became operational in 1963 with headquarters at Great Falls and missiles located in central and north-central Montana.

In 1964 Montana celebrated the centennial of the territory and the seventy-fifth anniversary of statehood. To kick off the year-long series of festivities, Senator Mike Mansfield sprinkled gold dust on the state's Tournament of Roses float, and Governor Tim Babcock fired a special frontier model of a Colt .45.

Montana gained stature in the winter sports world when the Missoula region was selected for the 1967 Winter Olympic trials.

A new state constitution went into effect in 1973, and the huge Libby Dam power project on the Kootenai River began operation in 1975.

THE PEOPLE OF MONTANA

Montana's Indian population of 27,130 reflects an increase of 6,000 between 1960 and 1970. The seven Indian reservations in operation today are the Blackfeet near Browning; Chippewa-Cree, Rocky Boy Reservation, Box Elder; Confederated Salish and Kootenai tribes, Flathead Reservation, Dixon; Crow, at Crow Agency; Fort Belknap Indian Community, Assiniboin and Gros Ventre, Harlem; Northern Cheyenne, Lame Deer; and Sioux tribes, Fort Peck Reservation, Poplar.

Over the years the Assiniboin filed claims against the United States government for taking their land. Finally they received a payment of $4 million to settle the claim. One of the most striking tribal dances is the Sun Dance of the Assiniboin, although during this dance they no longer practice self-torture.

All seven of the Indian reservations have market centers where the goods and crafts of the tribe are sold, such as the fine beadwork of the Crow. Many individual Indian artists and craftsmen will take orders for their art objects. Some tribes have tourist centers, like the Northern Cheyenne center at Lame Deer. However, Indian per capita income remains very low. Alcoholism and suicide rates on the reservations are the highest in the nation, and educational achievement is still very low.

A number of towns and cities of the state are known particularly for various nationality groups, such as the Irish, Welsh, and Italians of Butte; Belgians of Valier; French of Frenchtown; Finns of Boyd; and Russians of Seventynine.

Red Lodge is known as the "melting pot of Montana," because of its many nationalities. Its annual Festival of Nations is famous. It features exhibits and entertainment reflecting the various European cultures of the vicinity.

Montana's black population is among the smallest of all the states—only 2,000 in the 1970 census.

The state of Montana took an early interest in the welfare of its people. It was the first state to begin a system of old-age pensions and was almost the first to offer workmen's compensation.

The influences of the frontier, only a generation or two removed, and the pull of the great open spaces are still strong in Montana. Many Montanans continue to feel that any person who is unable to ride fifty miles in the saddle is somehow uneducated.

A story is told of a Montana sheepman named Smith who shot a grizzly bear and then was badly mauled by it. When the bear started to leave, Smith began to crawl away, only to have the bear come back, tear off a portion of his scalp, puncture his skin again and again with fierce, bone-deep bites in his legs, arms, and shoulders. When the bear finally departed, Smith, weak from loss of blood, crawled back to camp, climbed on his horse and rode to the nearest aid, then had to endure an 80-mile (129-kilometer) auto trip to the hospital. In spite of all this he was back on his ranch in short order.

This story is just another good indication of the strength of character and courage of both bears and Montanans.

Natural Treasures

MINERAL WEALTH

The region of Butte has been labeled "one of the richest mineral areas of the world." Despite the vast wealth already taken out of the region, it is estimated that billions of dollars worth of various minerals have yet to be removed. Many experts believe that the mineral wealth of the state as a whole has scarcely been touched.

Enormous coal reserves, especially in eastern Montana, have hardly been worked at all. There is an estimated reserve of 50 billion short tons (45,360,000,000 metric tons) of coal in Montana. The oil reserves are placed at 164 million barrels, and natural gas reserves are considered to be at least 900 billion cubic feet (25,479,000,000 cubic meters). Sweetgrass Arch is an important oil-bearing formation.

Granite and other stone, vermiculite, zinc, lead, corundum of gem quality found near Norris, and rubies are among the commercial minerals mined in the state. More gem sapphires are found in Montana than in any other state. Besides the cornflower blue sapphires of Yogo Gulch, green, red, and aquamarine sapphires are also found.

So many precious and semiprecious stones may be picked up that Montana is known as a rock hound's paradise. Montana moss agates are highly prized. Others include amethysts, amazonstones, garnets, jasper, white topaz, and quartz. Even diamonds have been reported at Greenhorn Gulch in Madison County, Grasshopper Creek in Beaverhead County, and Deer Lodge County.

TEEMING WITH LIFE

"Game is very abundant[;] we can scarcely cast our eyes in any direction without perceiving deer Elk Buffaloe or Antelopes," wrote Meriwether Lewis in describing Montana's abundance of wildlife. He estimated that within a circle of two miles (three kilometers) there were at least ten thousand buffalo. Only sixty years after Lewis saw the great herds of buffalo, the last big buffalo hunt was carried on in the state. It is likely that if the American Bison Society had not established the National Bison Range in 1909, there would be no buffalo left in Montana outside of zoos.

Lewis and Clark frequently encountered the ferocious grizzly bear. Clark wrote: "We saw a Brown or Grisley beare . . . killed the bear, which was verry large and a turrible looking animal, which we found verry hard to kill we Shot ten Balls into him before we killed him, & 5 of those Balls through his lights This animal is the largest of the carnivorous kind I ever saw." Lewis admitted frankly ". . . these bear being so hard to die rather intimedates us all; I must confess that I do not like the gentlemen and had reather fight two Indians than one bear."

Today, although the grizzly bear is thought to be on the way to extinction, it is possible that there are more grizzly bears remaining in Montana than in any other state except Alaska.

On April 29, 1805, Lewis wrote, "Capt Clark . . . informed me that he had seen a female and a faun of the bighorned anamal; that they ran for some distance with great aparent ease along the side of the river bluff where it was almost perpendicular. . . . "

The bighorn is a native of Big Horn Canyon, and a few of these rare and magnificent creatures still live in Montana. The fleet and agile Rocky Mountain goat might seem to be a relative of the bighorn, but actually it is not of the goat or sheep family at all; rather, it is a type of antelope.

Among the most unusual animals of Montana were the small number of white wolves of the Judith Basin. Old Snowdrift and his mate Lady Snowdrift became legendary. When their den was found, seven white pups were taken.

Game is still abundant in the state. Each year hunters bag deer, antelope, elk, bear, moose, mountain goats, and mountain sheep. There is an annual fur catch of beaver, badger, bobcat, coyote, red fox, lynx, marten, mink and muskrat, otter, raccoon, skunk, weasel, and wolverine. A million sportsmen annually hunt in the national forests of the state.

At one time, millions of buffalo grazed on the western plains of the United States. Most of the herds that are left today are protected by law.

There are twenty federal and eighteen state wildlife refuges in Montana.

Montana's wildlife includes 100 species of mammals, 350 of birds, 36 of amphibians and reptiles, and 86 species of fish. State officials claim that "no other state can approach these numbers."

One of the most unusual birds of the state is the Maximillian jay, first discovered by Lewis and Clark at their campsite near La Hood.

Sportsmen enjoy the pleasures of Montana's more than 4,000 miles (6,437 kilometers) of fishing streams. The second-largest brook trout ever caught was hooked near Three Forks. Among the prized game fish are the famous landlocked sockeye salmon.

One of the rare water creatures is the Axolotl salamander of Madison County. If its pools dry up it can adapt to living on land.

PLANT LIFE

More than two thousand species of wild flowers and plants thrive in Montana. These range from the dainty state flower—the bitterroot—to the deadly death camas. The bitterroot blossom is encircled by a kind of crown of twelve to eighteen leaves. After being in the sun a few days its pinkish flower changes to white. The root of this plant was used by the Flathead Indians as a pungent food, dried and eaten much as parsnips, pounded into powder, or mixed with pemmican or wild berries. It gives its name to the mountain range, river, and valley of the region where it was most common.

Some of the most spectacular alpine flowers are found along the upper reaches of the Beartooth Highway, which cuts through the primitive Beartooth region. Because of the altitude, growth is hindered; an entire alpine violet plant may grow no more than an inch (2.5 centimeters) high, with the most delicate of blossoms, and yet many areas are often carpeted with bloom of heather, alpine columbine, dryad, Rocky Mountain laurel, and others. This is the region of the famed "pink snows," caused by the tiny pink plants that grow on the surface.

In the Glacier National Park area alone, there are more than a thousand species of plants. Hundreds of other varieties bloom in the foothills and on the plains.

Much of the finest woodland in Montana is within the eleven national forests, covering 16,635,000 acres (6,732,000 hectares). Operated by the National Forest Service, Savenac Forest Nursery, which grows seedlings for reforestation, is the largest of its type in the nation.

Protecting the forests from fires is one of the most important services. At the Smokejumpers' Center in Missoula, visitors are welcome to visit the installation where crews are trained for forest fire fighting and dispatched by plane wherever fires threaten.

People Use Their Treasures

WEALTH FROM THE SOIL

In spite of the "glamour" of mining and the quick wealth sometimes possible from a rich mineral strike, the backbone of Montana's economy is still agriculture.

Agriculture brings more than one billion dollars of annual income to the state. Of this, about one third comes from livestock and about two thirds from crops.

The state is particularly proud of the fact that a large proportion of the farms and ranches in Montana are operated by their owners. The 90,000-acre (36,420-hectare) Thomas spread near Hardin has been called the world's largest wheat farm.

Great Falls considers itself the center of the state's wheat empire, and some of the world's finest spring wheat is grown by dry farming methods, without any irrigation. In some good years the wheat crop value has been greater than that of the total mineral output of the state.

Field stripping and farmstead windbreaks help protect the soil in west-central Montana's Cascade County.

Modern-day shepherd guides his flock. Wool is one of the state's leading livestock products.

Another crop is the evergreen; Libby calls itself the Christmas tree capital of the United States.

Some of the operations of farming and ranching are as lively and picturesque in modern times as they were in the old days. The annual calf roundup and the annual beef roundup still offer much of the old color. Few spectacles are more fascinating than sheep shearing, with its bleating cries and flying wool.

Montana ranks sixth among the states in wool production.

MINING AND MANUFACTURING

The yearly value of mineral production in Montana exceeds $600 million.

Among all the states, Montana ranks third in annual copper production—more than $100 million—but crude petroleum has dethroned copper as king with a value of $250 million. Coal, cement, sand, gravel, zinc, stone, silver, and lead are all important products. That most thrilling and exciting of the minerals—gold—does not even rank among the leaders.

Over the years the state has built up the mineral processing and refining industry. More efficient and ever larger smelters were built. Today the Washoe smelter of Anaconda Company is one of the world's largest. Montana processors were among the pioneers in the "flotation" process of refining. In this process pulverized ores are floated on water in which oil and certain chemicals have been placed. These catch the unwanted particles, making them sink to the bottom. The desired chemical floats on the bubbles at the top and is skimmed off in almost pure form. The process has been improved so that almost any desired mineral can be made to float on the surface in a process known as selective flotation.

One of the interesting by-products of mineral manufacturing is arsenic, which is recovered from the gasses of the many furnaces.

In another phase of industry, the first copper rolling mills west of the Mississippi were installed in the copper and zinc reduction works near Great Falls. As early as 1918 a cable and wire mill was completed at Great Falls, making the state active in every phase of metalwork, from mining of the ore to finished product.

Natural gas was first discovered in Montana at Glendive and the state's most important mineral, petroleum, was discovered in 1915 at Elk Basin. As of 1975, oil wells in the state produced more than thirty million barrels (over four million metric tons).

One of the "glamour" mining operations of the state is sapphire mining, at the Yogo Sapphire Mines of Yogo Gulch, not far from Garneill. These gems are found in shafts of clay, called pipes, in formations similar to those of South Africa's diamonds. Almost four years are required in the process of separating sapphires from the clay in which they are found. The smaller and less perfect stones become the jewels in better watches while the larger, purer stones are shipped to Switzerland or France to be cut and polished.

The manganese mines of Montana now produce much of the high-grade manganese of the country, and Montana leads in total production of the mineral.

A large amount has been added to Harvard University's vast endowment through the millions in gold hauled up by the Massachusetts institution's gold dredge on its holdings at Alder Gulch.

Manufacturing value in Montana has reached about $1.75 billion a year. Of course, much of the manufacturing income is based on processing the products of mines, forests, and farms, such as sugar beet refining, wheat flour milling, lumber milling, and furniture manufacturing. A large number of the state's products are also designed for use on ranches and in mines, such as mining machinery and the fancy saddles for which the state is noted.

TRANSPORTATION AND COMMUNICATION

The rivers, of course, were the first "roads" of Montana. Explorers, trappers, traders, and Indians made their way up them by paddling canoes, using the wind in light sailing craft, poling bull boats, or returning more easily with the current. Steamboats came as early as 1832, but they could not get very far into Montana because of the shallow water. By 1859, however, steamboats had been perfected which could "float on a damp sponge." The Missouri-Mississippi River system from the Gulf of Mexico to Fort Benton was opened to traffic.

Fort Benton became the most remote port on the mighty rivers and the hub of transportation for a vast region. Goods and passengers funneled into Fort Benton from all over the northern Rockies—by pack train, stagecoach, horseback, and even by camel caravan. Although the river passage was extremely long and winding and made dangerous by sandbars and snags, it was easy compared to the awful trials of the overland routes. Never before in the history of the world had such comfortable transportation been available so far into the interior of a continent.

Freight wagons and regular stagecoaches furnished most of the overland transportation for a long period.

Railroads first reached Montana in 1880 when the narrow-gauge Utah and Northern Railroad pushed up from the transcontinental railroad in northern Utah and reached Dillon; it had advanced to Silver Bow by 1881. In that same year the first transcontinental tracks crossed the eastern boundary of Montana and arrived at Miles City before construction was ended by winter weather. The last section to be finished was the hardest, lying across 300 miles (483 kilometers) of mountain. Long tunnels were bored under Bozeman

Pass and Mullan Pass. Shoulders of the mountains which could not be bypassed had to be blasted away.

Henry Villard, president of Northern Pacific, finally drove the last spike on September 8, 1883, about seven miles (eleven kilometers) from Garrison.

The next railroad to make the difficult crossing was the Great Northern, and much rivalry between the two railroads later arose.

The Milwaukee Road was the third great transcontinental railroad to serve Montana. It was the first railroad to have a long section using electric power. The complete 438-mile (705-kilometer) mountain division is electrified. The Milwaukee Road's route incorporated a part of the Central Montana Railroad. This was known as the "Jawbone line," because it was said to have been built mostly on "talk." For a time the Jawbone had little business; its president wrote: "There were no towns on the line, nor ... any provocation for towns, but ... I drew up a schedule and located ... plenty of them. Two young ladies (Fan and Lulu) were visiting at my house. On the timetable you will find ... Fanalulu just below ... Ringling."

Today's transportation system is a far cry from those primitive times. A network of superhighways, railroads, bus lines, and airlines serves Montana. Billings claims that it provides more airline service per capita than any other city in the United States.

Montana's first newspaper was a sheet printed at Virginia City in January 1864, and its name is not even known. The first substantial newspaper was the *Montana Post,* founded in August 1864, by publishers M.M. Manner and John Buchanan. In their first issue they modestly claimed, "We have correspondents in the various camps, who will keep our readers well posted on what is going on in ... our young and rapidly growing territory."

Their first edition of 960 copies was soon sold out, many of the buyers paying with a pinch of gold dust.

The *Anaconda Standard,* founded by copper king Marcus Daly in 1889, gained a nationwide reputation. Among its many pioneering achievements was the publication of one of the first full-color comic sections.

Sculpture of Charles M. Russell, the Montana artist whose work chronicled life in the West during the late 1800s. He is the only artist who has been honored by a place in Statuary Hall in the nation's Capitol.

Human Treasures

"MONTANA'S GREATEST INSTITUTION"

Only one artist in the country's history has been honored by a place in Statuary Hall in the Capitol at Washington, D.C., the government's Hall of Fame. This is Charles M. (Charley) Russell.

Born in 1864, Russell moved to the West as a boy; he came to know through experience the life of the region, having served as sheepherder, cowboy, hunter, and trapper. He knew the people, too—old-timers, fur traders, gunmen, and dance-hall girls.

The story is told of how he began to draw while working as a shepherd near Stanford. This was lonely and boring work. Some herders were so bored that they spent their time piling up rocks into cairns. These monuments to loneliness can still be seen. Russell used the colored clays around him to draw pictures of his surroundings. He became so absorbed in this that he once lost his herd.

Russell was much moved by the sufferings of the cattle during the awful winter of 1886-1887. When the absentee owner of the ranch where he worked wrote to inquire about his herds, Russell painted on an envelope a picture of a lonely range cow, dying of hunger, and a hungry coyote licking its chops nearby. He called it *Waiting for a Chinook (The Last of Five Thousand).* The foreman sent the picture to the owner, saying "That tells the story better than I can write it." This painting brought Russell his first fame as an artist, and for years the poignant picture was a favorite on picture postcards.

Russell's work was exhibited in London in 1914; he began to sell his paintings at rapidly advancing prices. His last unfinished work brought $30,000. The known works of Charles Russell include at least three thousand models, bronzes, sketches, watercolors, and oils, created with verve and vitality over a period of forty-six years. With great talent and intimate knowledge of the West, he painted authentic and exciting pictures. His paintings chronicle the sad passing of an era.

Russell died at Great Falls in 1926, and cowboy-humorist Will Rogers wrote a warm tribute to the man and his work.

Photographs of Russell and Rogers show that they were surprisingly alike in appearance, and many people said the same about their sense of humor.

OTHER CREATIVE MONTANANS

Another great painter of Indians and Western scenes was Frederic Remington. He went to Montana at the age of nineteen and there had "his first love affair with the West." The third famous Montana artist of Western subjects was Ralph de Camp.

Edgar S. Paxson spent twenty-one years in painting and research before finishing his renowned historical painting, a panorama showing as much detail as is known about Custer's Last Stand. J.R. Ralston is another Montana artist.

Among well-known Indian artists of the state are wood-carver John Clarke and sculptor Gary Sohildt, both Blackfeet.

Montana literary figures include Will James, cowboy author and illustrator; Mrs. B.M. Bower, author of the *Flying U* novels; and Max Miller, whose works include *I Cover the Waterfront.*

MONARCHS OF THE MINING COUNTRY

Marcus Daly came to Butte in 1876 as a representative of the Walker brothers of Salt Lake City to look into the purchase of the Alice silver mine. Later he bought the Anaconda claim and others, built the smelter at Anaconda, and became the father of the copper industry in the Butte area. One historian wrote: "Within twenty years Marcus Daly had become head of one of the world's most powerful monopolies, and a founder and builder of cities."

William Andrews Clark began as a storekeeper in Ophir City, expanded to wholesaling in Helena, branched out into other stores and banking, and then began investing in mining properties. By the time he was thirty-three he was a leading banker, merchant, and millionaire.

Daly and Clark were of quite different temperaments. Daly was called "warm, generous, gregarious." Clark has been described as "detached, arrogant, and uncompromising. It was said that not a dollar got away from him except to come back stuck to another."

At first these two men were friends; then they became rivals in an unending feud that often "embroiled most of Montana." In the fight to locate the state capital, Daly backed Anaconda, and Clark fought for Helena. Both spent huge sums for their own candidates.

Their greatest battle came when Clark set his sights on a seat in the United States Senate. He was opposed at every turn by Daly. At that time senators were chosen by the state legislatures. Clark was chosen but was accused of spending $431,000 to bribe legislators to vote for him, so he did not take his seat. He tried four times before he finally was able to serve his full term as senator. However, Daly was on his deathbed at this time.

Another prominent character of the mining region was F. Augustus Heinze, who, it was said, was determined to become a mining tycoon no matter what method he used. He employed as many as thirty-two lawyers to find legal means of getting the best of his competitors. Sometimes he had as many as forty court actions pending at one time. He was said to control the decisions of a Butte judge, William Clancy. His lawyers fought in the courts, while the miners fought underground. They used unslaked lime, boiling water, and dynamite.

Heinze sold out his Butte properties for $10.5 million in 1906. The 110 suits pending, involving claims for more than $70 million, were dismissed. Heinze went to New York, but there his schemes failed and he was practically bankrupt. He died in Saratoga, New York, at age forty-five.

IN THE PUBLIC EYE

A modern-day figure of national reputation in government is Mike Mansfield, for many years the Majority Floor Leader of the Senate. A Montana senator of a somewhat earlier period was Burton

K. Wheeler, who ran for vice president on the Progressive ticket of Robert M. LaFollette in 1924. After his loss, Wheeler continued in the Senate.

A Montana man, Frank Walker, served in the cabinets of Franklin Roosevelt and Harry Truman as postmaster general.

As the first woman in the Congress of the United States, Montana's Jeannette Rankin is assured of her place in national history.

Granville Stuart, a well-known cattleman of the Lewistown region, served as minister to both Uruguay and Paraguay; he later became a historian and writer.

America's chief World War I military man, General John J. Pershing, saw service at Fort Assiniboin in Montana.

One of Montana's military men who saw service both on the plains as a scout and in the Philippines and Alaska was Luther Sage (Yellowstone) Kelly—one of the intrepid immortals of the Western plains. He distinguished himself as a soldier, miner, hunter, trapper, guide, and scout.

Harold C. Urey, noted scientist, was a student and later a professor at the University of Montana. He won the Nobel Prize for chemistry in 1934.

One of the country's best-known television news commentators, Chet Huntley, was born at Cardwell. Actress Myrna Loy is a native of Radersburg.

SUCH INTERESTING PEOPLE

One of the most romantic persons of American history is the Indian woman Sacajawea, who lived with her people near the Three Forks until she was captured by the Minnetaree Indians and taken east with them. She married a French-Canadian trapper named Tuissant Charbonneau. Lewis and Clark hired the couple to be their guides. Charbonneau was something of a coward and not a very good guide, but Sacajawea proved fearless and constantly helpful. The couple's baby son Pomp was with them, and the members of the expedition grew very fond of him.

Mah-to-toh-pah, Mandan chief, painted by George Catlin.

Sioux medicine man, Sitting Bull, in 1890.

Crow Chief Plenty Coups.

Among the other prominent Indians of Montana were Three Eagles, chief of the Salish; Chief Gauche (Left Hand) of the Assiniboin; and Robert Yellowtail, superintendent of the Crow Reservation. He was the first Indian ever to head the administration of a reservation.

Last of the line of great Crow chiefs was Plenty Coups. During the ceremony of dedication for the Tomb of the Unknown Soldier at Arlington National Cemetery, Chief Plenty Coups represented the Indian nations as a head of state.

The community of Wibaux is named for Pierre Wibaux, who made a fortune in cattle, lost his fortune, and later owned as many as seventy-five thousand head of cattle. The story is told that a Chicago packing company made an agreement to buy from Wibaux a shipment of cattle at a given price. When the price of cattle went down, the company refused to go through with the deal. Wibaux sued; as witnesses he brought a large number of cowboys to Chicago. "Have a good time, boys," he urged. "Spend as much as you like; that company will pay for your entertainment." They painted the city a cow-country red, Wibaux won his suit, and the company paid the expenses of one of the largest groups of witnesses ever to testify.

St. Ignatius Mission, founded in 1864 by the Jesuits as a boarding school for Indians, as it looks today.

Teaching and Learning

The state of Montana supports a university system of six units, including the University of Montana, Missoula; Montana State University, Bozeman; Western Montana College, Dillon; Eastern Montana College, Billings; Northern Montana College, Havre; and Montana College of Mineral Science and Technology, Butte.

Classes at the University of Montana began in 1895 in temporary buildings. The first permanent buildings were occupied in 1899. Today the institution enrolls about eight thousand students.

Montana State University was the earliest unit of the university system to be established—February 16, 1893. Present enrollment is about nine thousand.

President William Howard Taft took part in the dedication of Mount St. Charles College at Helena in 1909. The name was later changed to Carroll College in honor of Bishop John P. Carroll, its founder.

The College of Great Falls was founded in 1932. It has recently completed a multimillion dollar expansion program on its 104-acre (42-hectare) campus.

The first European-style teaching in the state probably was done by the missionaries among the Indians. The first formal schools began in 1863 at Bannack and Nevada City. Lucia Darling, territorial Governor Sidney Edgerton's niece, was the teacher at Bannack and wrote an interesting description of the community: "tumultuous and rough, the headquarters of . . . highwaymen, and lawlessness and misrule seemed the prevailing spirit. . . . But . . . many worthy people . . . were anxious to have their children in school. I was requested to take charge."

Miss Darling held the classes in her own home, with the children using any books they happened to have. The school was forced to close for the winter because of the cold, but the twenty students returned in spring, and Bannack built a log schoolhouse the next summer that may still be seen there.

In 1864 the Jesuits of St. Ignatius began the first Indian boarding school in the Northwest.

The first territorial legislature in 1865 organized a system of schools, but compulsory education was not established until 1883.

In 1974-1975, an estimated 113,000 elementary students and 58,000 secondary students attended Montana's 839 schools. They were taught by an estimated 9,050 teachers.

One of the unusual research institutions of the state is the Rocky Mountain Laboratory of the U.S. Public Health Service, near Hamilton. In 1873 the first case of Rocky Mountain spotted fever was recorded in the Bitterroot Valley. Neither cause nor cure was known, and many deaths resulted. This was probably the greatest health menace in the whole western region. The Montana State Boards of Health and Entomology brought in scientists to a camp of tents, log cabins, woodsheds, and abandoned schoolhouses. By 1906 they had proved that the bite of a wood tick is the cause of the dread disease.

One of the triumphs of medical science was the development of a vaccine at the Rocky Mountain Laboratory. Yearly vaccination of those exposed to tick bites now effectively prevents the disease.

Today the laboratory is a modern institution where research is done on many infectious diseases that are problems in the West.

Enchantment of Montana

HIGH, WIDE, AND HANDSOME

What is Montana? It is great open spaces. It is forests. It is towering mountains and ski runs. It is a hunter's paradise and a land of trout streams. It is a view from the Continental Divide. It is a bustling, modern state where there are lingering echoes of creaking prairie schooners and ghosts of great buffalo herds.

Every visitor will discover his or her own special interest: more dude ranches than any other state except Arizona, more than a hundred ghost towns haunted with memories of the stirring past, a wealth of museums recalling the life of the frontier, the tepee rings (circles formed by stones to hold down the tepees)—only reminders of forgotten camps. There are also state parks, monuments, and recreation areas; the craft work of the Indians and the other local artisans; and many summer theaters with competent casts.

Others will find the greatest joys in the winter season, when the fish almost crash through the ice to jump at the hook. There are also notable winter carnivals, and the winter skiing is excellent. Winter sports resort areas are popular in Montana. The first United States luge run was built at Lolo Hot Springs, southwest of Missoula, and is sanctioned for Olympic competition. A luge (rhymes with rouge) is a one- or two-man bobsled course. Steered entirely by the body, the sled can reach a speed of 90 miles (145 kilometers) an hour.

West Yellowstone and Butte are well-known areas for snowmobiling, another popular pastime in Montana.

Scenery, of course, is everywhere—not only in the mountains but also on the boundless plains. Meriwether Lewis wrote of the endless scenes of enchantment. Now, the entire 1,940-mile (3,122-kilometer) route of Lewis and Clark through Montana is indicated by historical markers.

Opposite: Snowmobiling is among the many winter sports enjoyed by Montanans and visitors to the state.

NESTLED IN A PRICKLY PEAR: HELENA

Today a unique tourist "train" chugs along Main Street in Helena. It runs over historic Last Chance Gulch, where thousands of miners once grubbed and scrambled for wealth, some of which may still be buried beneath the concrete of the street. A most modern city has grown around the historic old gully, and its sights are best seen from the Last Chancer, in one of four gold carriages pulled by a replica of an engine. This "train," sponsored by the chamber of commerce, hauls tourists on regularly scheduled sightseeing tours of the city during the summer months.

Tourists see the crooked main street; legend has it that the many curves were made so there wouldn't be a long enough stretch for a good shot in the days of gunfights. The Last Chancer passes the Pioneer Cabin, built in 1865-1866; an old buffalo trail; the state capitol; and the Veterans and Pioneers Memorial building. This houses one of the finest historical museums in the West, including the famous collection of Charles Russell's works.

There are numerous other sights, including St. Helena's Cathedral, said by some to be "probably the most magnificent structure along the 1,500-mile parallel between Spokane, Washington, and the Twin Cities." There are also the famous Union Bank gold collection and the old fire tower, believed to be the only one left standing in the United States.

The famous Brewery Theater is gone, but plays are now produced at the Grand Street Theater, a former library and, before that, a church.

The state capitol is constructed of handsome Montana granite and surmounted by a classic dome; this is appropriately sheathed in copper. The interior is enlivened by the noted murals of Charles M. Russell, E.S. Paxson, and other artists. One of the Russell murals, the largest in the building, shows the meeting of Lewis and Clark with the Indians at Ross Hole. The various murals of the building are said to form one of the most notable collections in the West. A striking marble stairway ascends beneath a stained-glass ceiling and is lighted by a stained-glass window.

The state capitol in Helena (left) is constructed of Montana granite and is surmounted by a copper-sheathed dome. One of the murals inside the building is Lewis and Clark Meeting the Flatheads in Ross Hole, *by Charles Russell (below).*

Set in grounds of twelve and a half acres (five hectares), the capitol is surrounded by trees and shrubs of the state.

The modern ranch-style governor's mansion, completed in 1959, houses the chief executive a convenient two blocks from the capitol.

A fine view of Helena, in the Prickly Pear Valley, and the surrounding area may be had from Mount Helena.

Cruises on the Missouri River about fifteen miles (twenty-four kilometers) north of Helena in the launch *Sacajawea II* offer a thrilling view of one of the notable landmarks of America. Captain Lewis wrote about it: "The river appears to have forced its way through this immence body of solid rock . . . where it makes it's exit below has thrown on either side vast columns of rocks mountains high . . . from the singular appearance of this place I called it the *gates of the rocky mountains.*"

THE REST OF THE EASTERN SLOPE

The ride over the Beartooth Highway from Red Lodge to Cooke City is a most thrilling one. Some have gone so far as to label it "the most scenic mountain road in the world." As the majestic highway passes over countless switchbacks and curves, rising higher and higher until it seems to be completely surrounded by vast mountains, it is easy to understand such exclamations over its beauty.

One of the unique areas that can be visited from this road is Grasshopper Glacier. Black strips of various layers in the glacier on close inspection are seen to be layers of grasshoppers. The insects apparently fell and died there. More snows covered them, followed by succeeding layers of grasshoppers and snow. Scientists from all over the world visit this unique natural exhibit.

Silver Gate provides the northwest gateway to Yellowstone National Park. West Yellowstone and Gardiner are the other Montana entrances. All three are winter gateways to the park. One of the most fascinating tours anywhere is the winter tour of the park by fourteen-passenger heated snowmobile. The steaming vapors of the vents pluming from the white powder of the snow, the reflections on the snow of the glowing colors of the park, and the soaring steam of Old Faithful and the other geysers all leave an unforgettable impression—one entirely different from summer visits.

Only a narrow portion of the northern and western borders of Yellowstone Park actually fall within Montana's borders.

At Sunset Hills Cemetery near Livingston many noted people are buried. Lord and Lady Blackmore of England visited the area in 1872. When Lady Blackmore died, the lord purchased five acres (two hectares) of land as a cemetery, and his wife was buried there under a large pyramid monument. Henry T.P. Comstock is buried in the cemetery; he took his own life after he had spent the $10,000 he received for discovering the Comstock silver lode in Nevada, from which others took hundreds of millions. Not far away is the grave of pioneer trailblazer John M. Bozeman.

Bozeman, the community named in the pioneer's honor, is just to the west. Montana State University is especially noted for its outdoor museum, featuring petrified stumps and pools stocked with strange variations of rainbow trout.

Historic Three Forks recalls its chief claim to fame with the Missouri Headwaters State Monument, where there are many memories of the discoverers of this site—Lewis and Clark. A tourist camp now rests where the famous travelers once had their camp. Nearby is vast Lewis and Clark Cavern, third largest of its type in the country. Also near Three Forks is one of the many buffalo jumps, a cliff over which the Indians drove herds of buffalo to their deaths.

History's most tremendous placer gold find made Alder Gulch famous overnight. After $300 million in gold had been ripped from the earth and after the town of Virginia City, which had sprung up overnight, had served its term as capital city, the community fell into decay and became one of the most famous ghost towns in the United States.

Today it is a ghost town no longer. Under the direction of Charlie Bovey, Virginia City has come to life again. Thompson-Hickman Memorial Museum shows relics of the gold camps and mementos of the men who made them. The museum was a gift of wealthy William Boyce Thompson. Other museums include Rank's Drugstore, featuring an old-time shop, and the Bale of Hay Saloon, featuring a working collection of mechanical music makers, hurdy-gurdies, and stereopticon peep shows.

At St. Paul's Memorial Church the stained-glass windows are the work of Louis Comfort Tiffany.

Forlorn Boothill Cemetery still serves as a reminder that crime does not pay, with its graves of outlaws hanged by the vigilantes. Many of those outlaw deeds were planned at nearby Robbers Roost, the picturesque hangout of sheriff-turned-robber Henry Plummer and many of his gang.

Bill Fairweather, who discovered the gold of Alder Gulch, died at Robbers Roost and was buried in Boothill Cemetery overlooking the valley where he started the rush to riches. Fairweather was casual about his wealth and often scattered gold dust in the streets for scampering children to pick up. Later he tried his prospecting luck in Alaska but returned to Montana and died at age thirty-nine.

One of the interesting sagas of Virginia City's history concerns the second book published in Montana. The author was sixteen-year-old J.A. Hosmer, who told of his travels in the West. He printed the book himself on a hand press and wrote: "My readers will notice that in a great many places where there ought to be full stops, nothing appears but commas, my reason for that is, I had but one small font of type, and scarcely any capitals, one large 'W' was all of that letter I had."

A great tourist attraction is the Alder Gulch short-line railroad, an old-time steam train that puffs its way from Virginia City to New City, carrying entranced travelers.

Many visitors in the region go south to visit the site of the great earthquake of 1959 and Quake Lake, a creation of the "shocking" geological occurrence that changed the face of the region. The effects of the quake have been carefully described and marked for visitors.

Near Wisdom is the Big Hole Battlefield National Monument, maintained as a tribute to both the soldiers and Indians who died there. Here Chief Joseph was stunned by a surprise attack but rallied and made his escape. A short distance to the west is Chief Joseph

Pass, where the Indians crossed the Continental Divide a short time before the battle.

"RICHEST HILL ON EARTH": BUTTE

Like a cat, Butte seems to have many lives. It began when William Allison and G.O. Humphrey found placer gold in 1864 at Silver Bow Creek. Many prospectors came in, but by 1870 almost half the people had left. Then in 1875 the rich silver of William Farlin's Travonia Mine made Butte the silver city. With Marcus Daly's success the Butte region became the copper capital of the Americas. The region survived the almost complete shutdown of the 1930s depression, bounced back, and now is prospering in many fields.

Butte's claim to be perched on top of the "richest hill on earth" is backed by more than $5 billion worth of mineral riches that have poured forth from it in the amount of almost 500 million tons (454 million metric tons).

Leading metal processor of the region is the mammoth Anaconda Company. The original mine was given its name by discoverer Mike Hickey during the Civil War. He had been reading about how General Grant "encircled Lee like a giant anaconda." Since that time Anaconda has become one of the most familiar names of the region, as well as of the mining world.

Butte mines its ores both from giant open pits, fascinating to visitors, and from mines, one of which descends 5,293 feet (1,613 meters). The famed Berkeley Pit of the Anaconda Company is the largest open pit in the area.

The Montana School of Mines at the western end of the city is the only such school in the country located so close to substantial mining and smelting operations. It is especially noted for its Mineralogical Museum. This includes some mementos of Reno Sales, known as the "father of Butte geology."

The city takes its name from Big Butte, a volcanic cone to the northwest. Its history is not only of mines and ores but also includes many other interests. John Maguire had opened his Maguire Grand

Opera House as early as 1885, and a Tacoma, Washington, magazine wrote that it was "the finest . . . on the Pacific Coast outside of San Francisco." Many well-known performers appeared there.

The town of Anaconda, to the west, was started by Marcus Daly because its good water supply was especially suited for use in his smelters. The story is told that one day as he was surveying the location of the future city, he noticed a cow standing in the field and directed his engineers: "Main Street will run north and south straight through the cow."

The Anaconda Company plant at Anaconda, which boasts "the world's largest smokestack," has made history in the science of cop-

The Berkeley Pit (below) is the largest open-pit mine in the Butte area.

St. Mary's Mission in Stevensville

per smelting, and the plant is famous throughout the mining and metallurgical world. From a straggling tent town, Anaconda has grown to be a modern community, but retains all of the aggressive spirit of the pioneer days.

THE REST OF THE WESTERN SLOPE

Missoula is the metropolis of a large area of western Montana. Almost since the time of Lewis and Clark it has been a center of trade and a crossroads of transportation. It still is a leading trade center for the four fertile valleys nearby, and headquarters of the United States Forest Service region and the Montana State Forest Service. The Smokejump Headquarters for forest fire fighters fascinates Missoula's visitors.

The University of Montana is known as the "school with a mountain [Mount Sentinel] on its campus." It offers the splendid Historical Museum in its Fine Arts Building. The art museum was the first to be established in the vast area of Montana, Wyoming, Idaho, and the Dakotas. It also gained a reputation as the home of the prominent and widely circulated literary magazine *Frontier and Midland.*

Not far south of Missoula is Stevensville, site of famed old St. Mary's Mission.

For turning back the clock there is nothing better than exploring a genuine Montana ghost town. Many of the camps are quite decayed and weed-topped, crouching sadly among rusted and abandoned mining equipment. Surprisingly, some appear almost habitable, places from which the people just walked away. Elkhorn, Garnet, and Marysville are often visited.

The mine at the ghost town of Granite, near Philipsburg, was sometimes labeled "the richest silver mine on earth," although this is a considerable exaggeration. Its backers had ordered work halted, but the telegram failed to reach the workers before a dynamite blast uncovered a bonanza worth $40 million.

Thompson Falls, named in honor of famed geographer-explorer David Thompson, contains a monument to its namesake. The community is near Salish House, built by Thompson. The Indians were awed by the surveying instruments and the telescopes he carried, and called him Kookoosint ("man who looks at stars").

Kootenai Falls dashes about 200 feet (61 meters) down in a series of cascades. At this point, Thompson noted in his journal: "To this date we had meat of a few small antelope, but by no means enough to prevent us eating moss bread and dried carp, both poor, harsh feed.... We met two canoes, from which we traded twelve singed muskrats and two shoulders of antelope, thankful for a change from the moss bread."

Near Libby is Giant Cedars Nature Trail of the Kootenai National Forest, one of the country's finest stands of virgin cedars. To the east is mammoth Libby Dam.

Among the points of interest at Flathead Lake are several state parks and Wild Horse Island in the lake, home to a few residents and a private game reserve.

Kalispell is a focal point for a great mountain vacation area. One of its main industries is the shipment each year of more than a million and a half Christmas trees. Growing and processing of seed potatoes is another major industry of the city.

The Mission Range (opposite) is in northwestern Montana.

GLACIER NATIONAL PARK

Straddling the Continental Divide is one of America's outstanding natural wonderlands—Glacier National Park, with its sixty "living" glaciers of shoving, grinding, crunching masses of slowly moving ice.

Over spectacular roads and 500 miles (805 kilometers) of fine trails, visitors can visit unspoiled areas where they may enjoy a mid-summer snowball fight; revel in a multitude of wild flowers; fish without a license; study a living textbook in geology, botany, and zoology; or simply enjoy the unparalleled mountain grandeur.

"Fifty miles of the most spectacular scenery anywhere" is one description of breathtaking Going-to-the-Sun Highway, which

Gunsight Lake in Glacier National Park.

passes over Logan Pass with its 100-mile (161-kilometer) view in all directions. At Logan Pass is the unusual and informative Visitor Center. The roads of Glacier are banked high with snow, sometimes as late as July.

According to Blackfeet legend, Napi, the Old Man God of the Blackfeet, came to earth from his home in the sun to create the world and all of its creatures, including the Blackfeet. His route to and from the sun was by way of Glacier, giving the route the name Going-to-the-Sun. Blackfeet Glacier takes its name from the Indian tribe.

The largest building in the park is the Many Glacier Hotel. A similar impressive building is the Glacier Park Hotel, with its smooth log construction and huge log pillars inside. There is also a hotel at Lake McDonald, chalets at Granite Park and Sperry, and many camps.

Among the park's many individual attractions are the ice caves of Grinnell Glacier; the 2,000-foot (610-meter) Featherplume Falls, that seems to vanish into a cloud of mist before reaching the bottom; Weeping Wall, a cliff with water pouring down its face; vividly blue Ptarmigan Lake; and placid St. Mary Lake, with its tiny Wild Goose Isle. Some of the most beautiful spots in Glacier can be reached only by foot or horseback, including close-up views of the glaciers.

Those who enjoy the park should remember the work of naturalist and conservationist George B. Grinnell, who probably did more than anyone else to bring the region to public attention.

GREAT FALLS

The population of Great Falls has skyrocketed in the last ten years. It is the second-largest city in Montana. This is made even more significant by the fact that within the memory of living people it did not exist at all.

It was not until 1880 that a businessman from Minnesota, Paris Gibson, visited the area and thought that the power of the Great Falls made this a likely spot for an industrial town. He came back in 1883, platted the town, and named it for the falls. Silas Beachley stayed at the town site that winter and had a difficult time when Indians stole his only blankets and most of his supplies. A few buildings were constructed in 1884, and by 1888 the community was large enough to be incorporated. Meat packing, railroads, hydroelectric plants, and refineries soon helped to build the city.

The hydroelectric dams have caused the several falls to disappear, except during very high water. Meriwether Lewis would no longer be able to say, "... the water in its passage down ... brakes into perfect white foam ... from the reflection of the sun on the spray or mist ... there is a beautiful rainbow produced which adds not a little to the beauty of this majestically grand scenery."

Another early writer, Robert Vaughn, also gave a picturesque description of Rainbow Falls: "... the entire river, 1,200 feet wide, hurls itself over an unbroken rocky rim ... into a vast ... amphitheater where when the sun is shining, a rainbow spans the river from bank to bank."

One of the major attractions of Great Falls for visitors is the Charles M. Russell Gallery and Original Studio. Displayed here is the Trigg collection of Russell paintings. Also on exhibit is the collection Russell made of Indian and cowboy clothing and other items he used as props in his paintings. Russell's original log cabin where he worked at Great Falls for some years is now at this museum.

Few artists have ever aroused the admiration of their hometown people as did Charley Russell. During his life he was a well-loved and often-imitated figure, and his influence still is felt in the community. Russell is buried in Great Falls.

Not far from Great Falls stood Fort Shaw, once the "social center" of a large area. Here members of the orchestra trimmed the wicks of kerosene lamps that formed the footlights for the first performance of professional theater in Montana.

BILLINGS

Billings came into existence when the village of Coulson asked the Northern Pacific Railway too high a price for land. The railroad then

Cattle grazing on beautiful Montana ranch land.

started its own town and named it in honor of Frederick Billings, then president of the railroad. In only a few months it became a bustling metropolis.

Today, after many ups and downs, the thriving city is now Montana's largest, with more than 130 industries, in the center of a huge and wealthy agricultural district.

Black Otter Trail, a scenic highway, runs east along the rimrocks north of the city. This trail was named for a Crow chief, Black Otter, who is buried in a marked-off area. Nearby is Sacrifice Cliff, where the Crow braves threw themselves to their deaths hoping to appease the Great Spirit during a smallpox epidemic.

Boothill Cemetery holds the usual collection of outlaw graves. Here also is buried U.S. Marshall Muggins Taylor, who brought the news of the Custer massacre to the area and who kept the peace in Coulson. Major Luther S. "Yellowstone" Kelly is buried atop the rims, west of Chief Black Otter's grave. He died in 1938, after retirement as a government scout.

Overlooking the valley from a point just south of the airport is the statue *Range Rider of the Yellowstone.* This life-sized bronze of a cowboy and his horse was contributed by old-time western movie star William S. Hart, who posed with his horse, Paint, for the statue.

Near Billings is Indian Caves National Historic Site, where prehistoric markings may be viewed.

Yellowstone County Museum has a large assortment of relics of pioneer and Indian life. The main floor is furnished in the manner of a pioneer cabin. This is also the site of the privately owned General Custer Museum and Western Art Gallery.

One of the historic natural attractions of the region is Pompey's Pillar. This 200-foot-high (61 meters) rock formation on the Yellowstone River was climbed by William Clark on July 25, 1806. He named it for little Pomp, son of Sacajawea, a favorite of the whole company. Clark's inscription of his name is still visible there.

OTHER POINTS OF INTEREST

Few visitors can describe their feelings as they stand on the bleak, treeless prairie where General George Armstrong Custer and his 264 men were wiped out by the Sioux and Cheyenne.

By the time General Terry reached the area after his own bitter battle, the battleground was desolate; Comanche, a horse, was the sole survivor of the Custer forces. Terry had so many wounded to care for that he could only bury the officers in shallow trenches and partly cover the bodies of the enlisted men. Captain H.L. Nowlan kept a record of the location of the officers burial places.

The next year a burial detail from Fort Keogh found that animals had destroyed many of the bodies. The few remaining bones of

General Custer were sent to West Point for final burial. Other bones were buried in a common grave, where a monument was raised in which are carved the names of all those who gave their lives in the battle. Later, a commission attempted to locate the places where the men fell. It was able to place marble monuments in 209 of the probable locations.

Many artists, often with more imagination than fact, have painted the battle. However, artist Gayle P. Hoskins determined to re-create the action in a painting that was as authentic as possible. The result is an aerial panorama of the battle. A color print of this painting is helpful to the visitor for visualizing the struggle.

The Custer battlefield (below) is a bleak, treeless prairie.

These are among the many faces of Montana. Opposite page: Buffalo share a highway with a modern car and pickup camper and bighorn sheep pose in their artificial Rocky Mountain setting at the Smithsonian Institution. On this page: The ski lift at the Big Mountain ski area in Whitefish and a typical western Montana winter scene.

Near Hardin is the location of Fort Custer. The story is told that at the fort, theater director John Maguire presented a performance of the play *Captain John Smith,* using soldiers in the cast and Crow Indians for the Indians in the play. The great Chief Plenty Coups was in the audience. As the play went on, the Sioux slipped up and stole the Crow horses. There was great confusion as Plenty Coups and his men, some in costume, dashed off to retrieve their mounts.

The ruins of Fort C.F. Smith, the first army post in Montana, are also located near Hardin. This fort was built to protect travelers over the Bozeman Trail.

From Hardin, one can visit dramatic Big Horn Canyon, with its lake and 3,000-foot-high (914 meters) walls.

The town of Bridger was named in honor of Jim Bridger, one of the greatest frontiersman. His ability to guide parties where no one else could find the way and his knowledge of the ways of the wild and Indian culture have become almost legendary.

Bridger, surprisingly, obtained a set of Shakespeare's works and employed a boy, at the rate of $40 a month, to read to him. He memorized many of the lines and often quoted Shakespeare. After *Richard III* was read to him, he said, "No man could be that mean!" and tossed the volume into the fire.

Not far from Garneill are interesting ice caves with floors of thick solid ice.

Lewistown lies almost at the geographic center of the state. Montana State Fish Hatchery there is one of the largest in the Northwest. Nearby is Kendall, one of the mining communities (with Maiden and Giltedge) from which nearly $20 million in gold was obtained.

Historic Fort Benton, last point for steamboat transportation on the Missouri River, was named for Missouri Senator Thomas Hart Benton. Supplies received at Fort Benton were shipped to trappers and miners throughout the territory. Ruins of the old fort still may be seen.

One of the state's most interesting museums—the Museum of the Plains Indians—is on the Blackfeet reservation. The museum contains Blackfeet carvings and many other Indian displays, as well as those of prehistoric peoples.

The flags of both Canada and the United States fly over Sweetgrass, in Montana, and Coutts, in Alberta. The towns are official ports of entry on the long border.

Bear's Paw Battlefield State Monument, near Chinook, marks the final tragic battle and place of surrender of Chief Joseph and his Nez Percé Indians after their tremendous flight toward safety in Canada.

Havre (pronounced Hay-ver) is the market center for a large farming area, mostly of wheat and hay. It is also one of the principal division points of the Great Northern Railway, which has large diesel shops there.

Glasgow owes much of its present prosperity to the great Fort Peck Dam. The story is told that army engineers took the mayor of Glasgow out one day to point out a location on the Missouri River where they thought someday a dam might be built. "Why it would cost a million dollars," marveled the mayor. "Probably seventy-five million," replied the engineers. Work on the dam, the third largest in the world, began in 1933 and was completed in 1940.

Glasgow claims to hold the record for the number of different "boom" periods—opening of the Indian land, opening of another 18,000,000 acres (7,284,348 hectares), the Fort Peck Dam, and finally the growth of Glasgow Air Force Base.

Fort Peck Dam contains 125,500,000 cubic yards (95,951,652 cubic meters) of earth, sand, and gravel and 1,000,000 cubic yards (764,555 cubic meters) of rock. It is the world's largest earth-fill dam constructed by the hydraulic method. The Fort Peck Recreation Area and American Legion Hot Wells are attractions of the region. The Hot Wells are said to be similar to those of Warm Springs, Georgia.

The city of Fort Peck was planned as a community to house administrators and workers at the dam.

Jordan was once known as the "lonesomest town of the world." The telephone line and road to Miles City did not come through to the town until 1935. Today it is a prosperous and up-to-date little cow town.

Wibaux deserved its reputation as a rip-roaring town where cowboys often held their shootouts. One legend states that a town

Rodeos are popular events in the state.
Here a barrel rider tries his skill.

storekeeper was able to pave a sidewalk with the empty cartridge shells he picked up about the town.

Medicine Rocks is a grouping of sandstone buttes carved into spirals, caves, arches, pyramids, and other forms by the action of rain and wind. Theodore Roosevelt once called them "fantastically beautiful."

Miles City has the largest railroad shops between the Twin Cities and the West Coast. The Range Riders' Museum and Pioneer Memorial Hall exhibits materials of the open range from the time, and the Roundup and Range Riders' Reunion is held at Miles City each year. The United States Range Livestock Experiment Station and Fish Hatchery is near Miles City, as is old Fort Keogh, which has been rebuilt.

Montana is still an uncrowded state on the open spaces of the Great Plains. Rolling plateaus are cut by river valleys. Forest areas in the west give way to mountains that rise to the Continental Divide.

Today, farmlands, minerals, and forests are used wisely by the people of Montana, who appreciate the beauty of their state and realize its potential.

Handy Reference Section

Instant Facts

Became the 41st state, November 8, 1889
Capital—Helena, settled 1864
Nickname—The Treasure State; Big Sky Country; Land of the Shining Mountains
State motto—*Oro y Plata* ("Gold and Silver")
State bird—Western meadowlark
State tree—Ponderosa pine
State flower—Bitterroot
State stones—Sapphire and agate
State song—"Montana," music by Joseph E. Howard, lyrics by Charles C. Cohan
Area—147,138 square miles (381,086 square kilometers)
Rank in area—4th
Greatest length (north to south)—315 miles (507 kilometers)
Greatest width (east to west)—580 miles (933 kilometers)
Geographic center—Fergus, 12 miles (19 kilometers) west of Lewistown
Highest point—12,799 feet (3,901 meters), Granite Peak, Park County
Lowest point—1,820 feet (555 meters), Kootenai River at Idaho line
Mean elevation—3,400 feet (1,036 meters)
Number of counties—56
Population—721,000 (1980 projection)
Rank in population—43rd
Population density—4.9 per square mile (1.89 per square kilometer), 1980 projection
Rank in density—48th
Population center—In Cascade County, 48.3 miles (77.7 kilometers) southeast of Great Falls
Birthrate—15.8 per 1,000
Infant mortality rate—18.1 per 1,000 births
Physicians per 100,000—111

Principal cities—Billings	61,581	(1970 census)
Great Falls	60,091	
Butte-Silver Bow County	41,981	
Missoula	29,497	
Helena	22,730	

You Have a Date with History

1743—Verendryes crosses into Montana
1795—Yellowstone River named
1805—Famed expedition of Lewis and Clark across Montana
1806—Lewis and Clark return
1807—Manuel Lisa builds trading fort at junction of Bighorn and Yellowstone rivers
1810—Menard and Henry build post
1822—William Ashley Company begins trading
1837—Indians stricken with smallpox
1841—Father De Smet founds St. Mary's Mission
1842—Montana's first crop is planted
1852—François Finlay finds modest amounts of gold at Gold Creek
1859—First steamboat reaches Fort Benton
1862—John White makes first important Montana gold discovery at Bannack
1863—Virginia City springs up around Alder Gulch bonanza; John M. Bozeman blazes his trail.
1864—Montana Territory organized; beginning of Helena at Last Chance Gulch
1866—First Texas cattle drive
1876—George Armstrong Custer defeated, slain at Little Bighorn
1877—Battle of the Bear's Paw
1880—First railroad reaches Montana
1883—Northern Pacific Railroad completed across Montana
1893—Montana State University founded
1895—University of Montana holds first classes
1906—Wood tick isolated as cause of Rocky Mountain spotted fever
1907—First major reclamation project completed
1909—National Bison Range established
1910—Glacier National Park created
1915—Petroleum discovered at Elk Basin
1916—Jeannette Rankin from Montana elected as nation's first congresswoman
1926—Artist Charles M. Russell dies
1938—Going-to-the-Sun Highway completed
1959—Earthquake causes wide damage in region near Yellowstone National Park
1964—Montana celebrates territorial centennial
1965—Mineral production reaches record peak value of $232,741,000
1967—Winter Olympic trials held in Montana
1973—New state constitution goes into effect
1975—Libby Dam project begins operation

Thinkers, Doers, Fighters

People of renown who have been associated with Montana

Bozeman, John M.
Bridger, Jim
Clark, William
Clark, William Andrews
Clarke, John
Colter, John
Custer, George Armstrong
Daly, Marcus
De Smet, Pierre Jean
Gauche (Chief)
Grinnell, George B.
Huntley, Chet
James, Will
Joseph, the Younger (Chief)
Kelly, Luther S. (Yellowstone)
Lisa, Manuel
Lewis, Meriwether
Mansfield, Mike
Miles, Nelson A.
Miller, Max
Plenty Coups (Chief)
Rankin, Jeannette
Remington, Frederic
Russell, Charles M. (Charley)
Sacajawea
Sitting Bull
Thompson, David
Three Eagles (Chief)
Urey, Harold C.
Walker, Frank
Wheeler, Burton K.

Territorial Governors

Sidney Edgerton 1856-1866
Green Clay Smith 1866-1869
James M. Ashley 1869-1870
Benjamin F. Potts 1870-1883
J. Schuyler Crosby 1883
B. Platt Carpenter 1883-1885
Samuel T. Hauser 1885-1887
Preston H. Leslie 1887-1889
Benjamin F. White 1889

Governors of the State of Montana

Joseph K. Toole 1889-1893
John E. Rickards 1893-1897
Robert Burns Smith 1897-1901
Joseph K. Toole 1901-1908
Edwin L. Norris 1908-1913
Sam V. Stewart 1913-1921
Joseph M. Dixon 1921-1925
John E. Erickson 1925-1933
Frank H. Cooney 1933-1935
W. Elmer Holt 1935-1937
Roy E. Ayers 1937-1941
Sam C. Ford 1941-1949
John W. Bonner 1949-1953
J. Hugo Aronson 1953-1961
Donald G. Nutter 1961-1962
Tim Babcock 1962-1969
Forrest H. Anderson 1969-1973
Thomas L. Judge 1973-

Index

PICTURE CREDITS

Color photographs courtesy of the following: Travel Promotion Unit, Montana Department of Highways, 2-3, 12, 15, 17, 28, 35, 36, 51, 58, 63 (right), 64, 66, 69, 74, 75, 76, 81, 83, 85 (top), 88; USDI, NPS, Fort Vancouver National Historic Site, 27; Western History Department, Denver Public Library, 31; Woolaroc Museum, Bartlesville, Oklahoma, 39; H. Earle Clack Memorial Museum, 42 (top); Gilcrease Institute, 42 (bottom); USDA, Soil Conservation Service, 53, 85 (bottom); USDA, Robert Hailstock, 54; Library of Congress, 63 (middle); USDI, NPS, Glacier National Park, 78; Thermopolis-Hot Springs Chamber of Commerce, 84 (top); Washington Area Convention and Visitors Association, 84 (bottom).

Illustrations on back cover by Len W. Meents.

ABOUT THE AUTHOR

With the publication of his first book for school use when he was twenty, **Allan Carpenter** began a career as an author that has spanned more than 135 books. After teaching in the public schools of Des Moines, Mr. Carpenter began his career as an educational publisher at the age of twenty-one when he founded the magazine *Teachers Digest.* In the field of educational periodicals, he was responsible for many innovations. During his many years in publishing, he has perfected a highly organized approach to handling large volumes of factual material: after extensive traveling and having collected all possible materials, he systematically reviews and organizes everything. From his apartment high in Chicago's John Hancock Building, Allan recalls, "My collection and assimilation of materials on the states and countries began before the publication of my first book." Allan is the founder of Carpenter Publishing House and of Infordata International, Inc., publishers of *Issues in Education* and *Index to U. S. Government Periodicals.* When he is not writing or traveling, his principal avocation is music. He has been the principal bassist of many symphonies, and he managed the country's leading non-professional symphony for twenty-five years.